ADVERTI[SING]

DOLLS

The History of American Advertising Dolls from 1900-1990

Myra Yellin Outwater

Photography by Eric Boe Outwater

Schiffer Publishing Ltd

4880 Lower Valley Road, Atglen, PA 19310 USA

Dedication

To my husband Eric, who became a photographer and book editor out of love; to my children Laurence, Andrew and Alexander, who valiantly struggled to eat enough hamburgers, cereals, candies and Klondikes to give their mother box tops, and to Charlie Schalebaum, who helped me ferret out so many of my treasures. Thank you.

Acknowledgements

To Althea and Pierce Randall and Elizabeth Martz for helping me in my search.

To Peter J. Blum and Dr. James Kintzel for their photographic help.

To the memory of Joleen Robison and Kay Sellers, whose book, "Advertising Dolls," remains the bible of all advertising doll collectors and the inspiration for this book.

To Colleen Oglesby for her help with the tedious job of proof reading.

And to Charlie the Tuna, Chiquita Banana, the Jolly Green Giant and Cracker Jack, thanks for all the fun, the memories and the good times. Entering a roomful of smiling doll faces is the best prescription for happiness.

Published by Schiffer Publishing Ltd.
4880 Lower Valley Road
Atglen, PA 19310
Phone: (610) 593-1777; Fax: (610) 593-2002
E-mail: schifferbk@aol.com
Please write for a free catalog.
This book may be purchased from the publisher.
Please include $3.95 for shipping.
Try your bookstore first.

We are interested in hearing from authors
with book ideas on related subjects.

Contents

Introduction

How Much Is It Worth? A Value Analysis

As in all collectibles pricing guides, value is relative and is determined by condition, scarcity, and demand. We have tried to give approximate values, but the final price is always determined in the marketplace, based upon what the dealer or consumer is willing to pay. Dolls in mint condition or in the original box or with the original accessories bring in a higher price than the same doll in a used condition. Older dolls from the early 1900s bring higher prices despite their condition because of scarcity. Dolls that cross categories such as antique cloth dolls, black dolls, fast food collectibles, 1940s and 1950s composition and hard plastic dolls, and Christmas collectibles often bring in higher prices than others in the same doll category.

As in all areas of collectibles, it is also important to remember geography. For example a doll like the Allentown, Pennsylvania, Alfundo the clown, has more value to someone who knows of Dorney Park than to someone unfamiliar with the doll's history.

The Birth of a Collector

I decided to collect advertising dolls in the 1980s as a lark. I had written an article, "Collecting on $25 or Less," and was looking for a cheap collectible that would provide me an adventure in collecting without draining my pocketbook. In a sense, I was ahead of the market. In those days I bought most of my advertising dolls for a few dollars. Today many of these same dolls cost considerably more. A doll I bought for $2 then in what I call the halcyon days of collecting today costs about $25. Another doll I bought for $105 now sells for more than $200.

At first I scouted out dolls in flea markets, collectibles shows and by buying boxes of cereal and hundreds of hamburgers. My collection grew rapidly as I happily bought dolls for $2 and $3. When my collection overflowed a small kitchen shelf, I knew I was hooked.

My first purchases were simple, a Ronald McDonald, a Burger King and a Levi Strauss doll, but soon my collection escalated into the next plateau and I was going after dolls in the $25 to $50 range — the Toni dolls, the Miss Revlons and black dolls such as Aunt Jemima. By this time I was a hunter, fascinated not just by the dolls but by the history of these advertising premiums. As I ferreted out more dolls, I began to search for and acquire the more expensive antique varieties, the cloth dolls of the early 1920s and 1930s — Lena, Anty Drudge, the Buddy Lees, and the Gerber Baby.

Today my collection numbers in the eight hundreds and is still growing. This year I found the original 1944 Kellogg's Chiquita Banana and one of my earliest dolls, the 1899 Miss Flaked Rice. Since I first began collecting advertising dolls, the older dolls have enjoyed more attention from both collectors and dealers. Baby boomers have re-discovered the dolls of the 1950s and advertising doll collectors must vie with other memorabilia collectors for the Coca Cola dolls, the Miss Revlons, the Toni dolls and all the fast food dolls — Ronald McDonald, Burger King and the Big Boys.

Although the advertising doll market has grown in the public's awareness since the 1970s, the use of these dolls as advertising vehicles is not a new phenomenon. My earliest dolls are Miss Flaked Rice, who was distributed in 1899, and a Singer Sewing Machine doll circa 1905 that was aimed at the German export market.

Unlike the advertising dolls of today, which carry the names of their products, the earliest advertising dolls had such names as Dolly Dimple, Flossie Collingbourne, and Trena.

It is interesting that, in seeking some of the older dolls, I entered the arena of the specialized doll dealer. The Quaker Crackels boy, which dates from 1924, is more frequently found in antiques shops than in doll shops. Aunt Jemima, Uncle Mose, and the Cream of Wheat man are considered Black Americana. The Coca-Cola Santa Claus is not only a Coca-Cola collectible but a Christmas collectible. Mr. Peanut and the Campbell Soup twins have their own dedicated fans.

Cloth dolls have been promoting American products since the late 1890s, when smart businessmen understood that a toy in daily use was an excellent advertisement for their products. And long before the days of the Madison Avenue gurus, business recognized that the way to a parent's pocketbook was through an appeal to their child.

In the early 1900s, companies began to realize the advertising potential of cloth dolls, not only as economical tools and attractive playthings, but as a practical vehicle to create national exposure for their products. In the days before radio and television, business managers knew that a simple trademark or a popular figural item could provide recognition and make their product a household name.

The first dolls were either given away with the product or cost a few cents in stamps to cover mailing. It didn't take long to realize the advantages of connecting the purchase of a soap, a cleanser, a cereal, or a soup with a giveaway plaything. Following the turn-of-the-century popularity of low-cost, mass-produced cloth dolls, businesses were delighted to piggyback on the success of these cuddly dolls and create new dolls for the growing market.

W.K. Kellogg Company was one of the earliest companies to capitalize on this premium offer phenomenon. The company created its first premium doll in the 1920s. Its unprecedented success soon convinced management that they had a winner, and for the next 60 years, the company would unleash a flurry of dolls and animal figures.

Advertising Kellogg's cereals with animals began with a flourish in the 1930s with Freckles the Frog, Crinkle the Cat, Dandy the Duck and Dinkey the Dog. One of Kellogg's most popular doll groups was the three jolly elves, Snap, Crackle, and Pop. Tony the Tiger and Froot Loops Sam came later. Today there is no place in the nation where Tony the Tiger goes unnoticed.

It wasn't long before other brands of cereal jumped on the doll bandwagon. Quaker Oats had Cap'n Crunch, Ralston Purina had the Raisin and the Scarecrow, and General Mills produced Trix the Rabbit, Count Chocula and Honey Bee.

It wasn't just cereals — sugars, candies, breads, and fast-food restaurants began creating dolls out of their trademarks. Gradually dolls such as Aunt Jemima and the Cream of Wheat Rastus would become American folk art collectibles.

Beginning in the 1940s and 1950s, advertising agencies stepped into the picture. In a move that predated the 1970s action figure craze of superheroes such as Superman, Batman, and G.I. Joe, they created unisex toys for both boys and girls. Ad agency designers went to work to create such friendly little people as the Brach's Candy Scarecrow Sam, Mohawk Carpeting's Tommy and Jack Frost Sugar Company's Jack Frost. Before long, Mr. Peanut, Ronald McDonald, Pillsbury's Doughboy, and Burger King would become not only trademarks but pop icons.

Some of these figures even developed voices and personalities that would go beyond the printed page, such as Chiquita Banana's song with its catchy Caribbean rhythms, the infectious beat of the hip California Raisins and the cool, streetwise voice of Charlie the Tuna. And what could be more inspired than the onomatopoeia of Rice Krispies' Snap, Crackle, and Pop?

In the years since, other companies have successfully impressed their corporate image on the American consciousness with trademark dolls. Since 1904, the sight of the chubby little Campbell Twins have become synonymous with soup. Since the early 1920s, the RCA Nipper, the little white dog with a cocked ear, suggests gramophones; and the mere sight of a Ronald McDonald or a Burger King creates a subliminal hunger for hamburgers.

Today premiums have become a universal marketing tool. Walk through any supermarket aisle and you find doll faces and fanciful animals on packages of cereal, cupcakes, toilet paper, and soap. Tony the Tiger, the Froot Loops Toucan, the Northern Toilet Paper Dolls, Tasty the Tastykake Baker, and Little Debbie are only a few. Move further along and meet the Sun Maid Raisin girl, the Morton Salt girl, and the Chicken of the Sea Mermaid. On other shelves the California Raisins sing out, M&M critters dance, and Pillsbury Doughboys pop out of their cans.

Advertising dolls are not just visual product reminders, but arbiters and bellwethers of fashion trends. They reveal changing American attitudes toward women and blacks. The Revlon dolls and the Betsy McCall and Harriet Hubbard Ayer dolls of the 1950s show how women's fashions changed, leading the way to the 1960s' breakthrough of the Barbie doll.

In fact, these dolls from the 1950s have become wonderful relics of the glamorous fifties and a favored collectible by those "grown-ups" who dream of reliving the days of their childhood. Said one doll dealer recently, "Adult men and women who try to buy back their childhood toys are some of our best customers."

The Revlon dolls were a dazzling symbol of idealized adult beauty and a preview of a glamorous life ahead. These dolls were a young girl's dream: Not only did they wear elaborate party dresses with pinched-in waists, but they were dressed in grown-up underwear, bras, nylon stockings with seams, girdles, and jewelry. In addition, the dolls wore lipstick and nail polish and had small breasts, the most important and visible symbol of adult femininity.

Today, once well-known trademarks dolls such as the Birdseye Trio, Anty Drudge, Buster Brown, and Aunt Jemima's husband, Uncle Mose, have faded into obscurity. Other doll trademarks such as the Toni Doll, Harriet Hubbard Ayer, the Miss Revlons, Betsy McCall, and Buddy Lee have become victims of changing times. Few today remember the agonies of a home permanent. Not many remember following Ayer's nightly regime of cold creams. Few keep up with fashion by creating their own wardrobe of McCall's easy-to-sew patterns. And few workers buy special jeans for work, as did the old customers of Lee Jeans.

But fortunately others remain. The Jolly Green Giant still sings "Ho Ho," and who hasn't succumbed to the irascible charm of Charlie the Tuna? Sorry, Charlie!

Advertising dolls appear in almost every industry and represent almost every profession. But one of their busiest times is Christmas.

The Christmas show began in the thirties when Coca Cola revamped the image of Santa Claus and created its own version of the venerable Christmas Saint. Today Christmas remains one of the biggest times for doll premiums. It is hard to escape the cuddly pleas of plush teddy bears to buy gasoline, bank CDs, or news magazines. Even department stores and supermarkets sell Christmas teddies. McDonald's, Wendy's and Burger King know that their hamburgers sell better when a small doll or action figure is available with the meal, and what better time to hype their product than at Christmas, a time when weary parents are seeking to escape the kitchen. Even Disney characters and popular cartoon and action figures appear at holiday seasons to help promote the fast food restaurants.

Today dolls are star players in the advertising campaigns of almost every major food company. They appear on television, on the radio, and in magazines. Ronald McDonald, Burger King, the Jolly Green Giant, Cracker Jack, Big Boy, and the Tony the Tiger are just a few of the many faces that sell corporate America worldwide on television, radio, billboards, magazines, and newspaper pages.

There is nothing as cheery as a room full of these smiling faces. Unlike the real world, the world of advertising dolls is one of constant smiles and good cheer.

My first purchases were a Ronald McDonald ($15), a Burger King ($10), and a Levi Strauss doll.($25) These are the most common dolls around and lulled me into a false sense of security that collecting these dolls would be easy. In one year the Chase Bag Company manufactured more than one million Ronald McDonald dolls, making this the most popular doll in America.

6

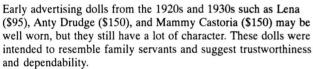

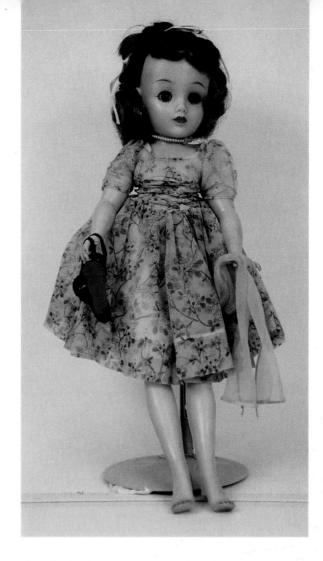

Early advertising dolls from the 1920s and 1930s such as Lena ($95), Anty Drudge ($150), and Mammy Castoria ($150) may be well worn, but they still have a lot of character. These dolls were intended to resemble family servants and suggest trustworthiness and dependability.

My collection became more expensive when I started to buy Miss Revlon dolls and found that I was competing with the baby boomers. ($200-250)

The Singer Sewing Machine doll ($150), c. 1905, was produced for the German Export market. She wears an ethnic German costume and is identified by the "S"' on her apron and the word "Singer" on her bonnet. The designer took pains with the details of her costume and tried to make it as authentic as possible. Notice the flowers and details of her skirt.

The Singer doll was designed to resemble other similarly costumed dolls, like this handmade doll from Eastern Europe. ($100)

The Quaker Crackels boy ($250) is not only a highly sought after advertising doll, but an early twentieth century American collectible.

Again, these dolls are of the ilk Singer hoped to emulate.

Kellogg was one of the first companies to create friendly animal and imaginary pals as trademarks. Snap, Crackle, and Pop were created in 1928. Their most famous modern image has been Tony the Tiger. ($35)

E.J. Brach Candy Corp.'s Scarecrow Sam. ($25, or $30 with book)

Jack Frost. ($25)

Clowns have always been popular toys for both boys and girls, and one of the most popular of all times has been Ronald McDonald.

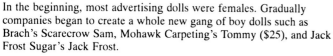

In the beginning, most advertising dolls were females. Gradually companies began to create a whole new gang of boy dolls such as Brach's Scarecrow Sam, Mohawk Carpeting's Tommy ($25), and Jack Frost Sugar's Jack Frost.

Advertising dolls have their ties to the music world, as well, with tie-ins with advertising jingles. In the 1940s everyone sang Chiquita Banana's ($20) tune and, in the 1980s, the California Raisins' ($10) theme song, "I Heard It Through the Grapevine."

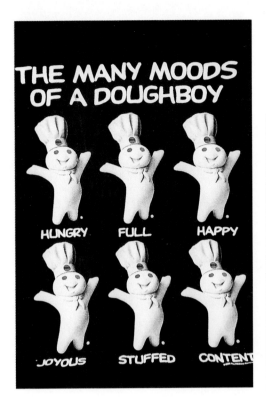

Enterprising ad agencies were quick to realize the popularity of animated trademark products such as Mr. Peanuts ($20) and the Pillsbury Doughboys. ($20)

Throughout their history, dolls have been fashion role models for young girls. In the 1950s, a popular fashion doll was this dainty little Miss Revlon. ($220)

Toucan Sam ($20) is another example of how Kellogg's animators created a lovable animal pal.

"Sorry Charlie," but I never heard of a talking fish before you swam ashore. ($25-$55)

You can never have enough Teddy Bears. From banks to magazines to gas stations, everyone makes room for a Christmas Teddy.

Chapter 1

Martha Jenks Chase Paves the Way for Cloth Advertising Premiums

Historians have documented the existence of small, doll-like figures in societies dating back as far as ancient Egypt. In fact, small, doll-like figures have been a part of every society and reflect the different costumes and faces of almost every people in the world.

Primitive cultures created small forms to use as fertility figures, ritual fetishes, and ceremonial or religious icons. Later men and women fashioned small figures out of straw, bones, wood, cloth, paper, dried fruit, and even old tools.

In our own country, Native Americans made dolls out of twigs. Colonial mothers made rag dolls out of bits of cloth and old clothes.

Later, more developed societies created an art form out of making human figures and these doll-like figures became decorative and ornamental objects for the home and the church. But it wasn't until the eighteenth and nineteenth centuries that craftsmen and doll makers began to create realistic doll-ladies, more like the dolls we know today.

The Industrial Revolution changed society's lifestyle. Suddenly adults were finding that they had leisure time and many chose to spend this time in more family oriented and home-centered activities. Mothers and fathers began to make small playthings for their children — carved wooden toys for the boys and simple rag dolls for the girls.

In the late 1890s, Amish women would sew rag dolls for their children without faces, in keeping with Deuteronomy (5:8)'s prohibition against making a graven image. The Swartenruber cult, one of the stricter observers of the Bible, made armless and legless dolls to further adhere to this injunction.

The Japanese have been among the most prolific doll makers in the world. In fact, even today there are several cities outside of Tokyo where the main industry is doll making. The Japanese carve dolls out of wood, weave figures out of grass and straw, and make graceful dancers out of handmade paper. Daruma dolls, which are armless and legless, symbolize Buddha's religious influence. An old legend says that the deity was so engrossed in his religious study that his limbs atrophied from lack of activity.

Few thought of dolls as frivolous playthings before the twentieth century. During the 1700s and 1800s, upper class girls were allowed to "play" with elegantly dressed dolls made out of bisque, porcelain, and glass. But unlike the dolls of the twentieth century, these dolls were more to be admired than cuddled, and because of their fragile natures they weren't considered active playthings.

But while manufactured dolls were in existence in the eighteenth and nineteenth centuries, they were the property of only a few privileged children. And doll play, a creative playtime activity, didn't become part of society's patterns until the late nineteenth century when the mass manufacture of cloth dolls made them available to almost every child.

The most common form of homemade dolls has always been rag dolls. And the most famous brand in the twentieth century has been Raggedy Ann and Raggedy Andy. These dolls became very popular in the early 1900s. The name Raggedy refers to the fact that they were sewn together from bits and pieces of old rags made from worn clothes and quilts. Raggedy Anns and Andys have remained one of the most popular and most copied dolls in America. Raggedy Anns and Raggedy Andys began life as a cartoon illustration created by Johnny Gruelle.

All doll makers know that little girls love to play with their dolls' hair. It is interesting to note that yarn has been the most popular material for the hair of cloth dolls. The hair of Raggedy Anns and Andys are usually made of red yarn. Blond has been the most popular color in recent times and, with the exception of the 1973 Levi Strauss boys, which have red yarn wigs, most cloth dolls of the 1960s, 1970s, and 1980s — such as the girl Levi Strauss dolls, the Mattel Shoppin' Pals, Chicken of the Sea, Cracker Jack, the Morton Salt Girl, the Swiss Misses, and the Sunbeam girls — have had lush-yellow yarn wigs.

By the late 1800s parents, educators, and clergy began to understand the value of dolls as educational teaching tools. New England educator and child psychologist G. Stanley Hall discussed the instructional value of doll play in his book, "A Study of Dolls," in 1896. He wrote that dolls were intended to nurture maternal, feminine instincts, teach young girls useful accomplishments, and act as role models for idealized female dress and decorum.

Hall was not alone in his thinking. Society was more religiously oriented then. And many believed that idle hands were devil's play and children should not be allowed to have long hours of leisure. Children were considered "adults in waiting," and most of their activities were focused on learning and acquiring skills that would profit them well as adults. Even the privileged children of the upper classes were supervised almost every hour of the day. Walks and horseback rides were sandwiched in between hours of music, art, and language lessons. Middle-class children were encouraged to learn to read, write, sing, and play an instrument. Music and art lessons were often considered necessary social skills in an age when home entertainments were mainly amateur musicales. Working-class urban and rural children also had little idle time. City children were expected to do chores at home and become apprentices at an early age in trades and at factories. Farm children worked in the house and the fields to help contribute to the economic survival of their families. Young farm boys learned to plant, tend the animals, hunt, and fish; young girls to sew, bake, and clean.

The nature of doll play changed dramatically in the mid-nineteenth century when women like Izannah Walker and Martha Jenks Chase set up home factories to mass produce cloth dolls and compete with the European doll makers in Germany, France, and Italy.

Before the advent of the cloth doll, most "bought" dolls were elaborate constructions of porcelain and bisque, dressed in exquisite lace, satin, and ribbons. And because they were so fragile, they became Sunday toys intended to be used only as an after-church activity. Cloth dolls invited play. Unlike the French and German porcelain and bisque dolls that were usually the property of more affluent children, cloth dolls were inexpensive. The French and German dolls had heads that could break. Cloth dolls were child proof, almost indestructible. Even the worst accidents could usually be remedied with a needle and thread.

The New England doll industry began in 1840 in an unlikely setting, the home of Izannah Walker, a young Rhode Island homemaker. When Walker began to make dolls, she had no idea that her dolls would mark the beginning of a new movement that would democratize doll play and make dolls available to the average child.

Walker's simple, cloth doll with its oil-paint face would eventually bring about a revolution in play. But when Walker produced her first few dolls, the event was barely noticed, nor would it have far reaching ramifications until a daughter of one of her friends, Martha Jenks Chase improved on Walker's idea and created the Chase doll, a cloth doll with an oil-painted face that looked just like a real child.

Chase's first dolls were hand painted, waterproof, jointed stockinette dolls and much more lovable compared to the smooth-faced dolls with their fragile heads and bodies being imported from Europe. While the more formal bisque dolls invited respect, these huggable cloth dolls invited love and affection. It was in these cloth dolls that young girls found not only a plaything but a secret friend. Like many women doll makers, Chase preferred soft-bodied dolls that were cuddly to touch compared to the dolls with mechanical parts created by male doll makers. Chase believed that dolls should invite cuddling and emotional rapport.

Like many mothers of her day, Chase recognized the joy of playing with dolls and often made homemade dolls for her own seven children. As a young adult, she had championed the new theories of "child study" and "scientific

mothering." Chase believed that dolls should be designed to promote the emotional and educational well-being of young girls and prepare them for their future roles as mothers. In addition, Chase felt that cloth dolls offered an alternative to the European fashion dolls, which she felt encouraged young women to be materialistic and indulge in conspicuous consumption.

The M.J. Chase Company was officially established in 1889. By the 1890s, Chase, the daughter and wife of a physician, had created a cottage industry of women cutting and sewing a line of dolls that would become the first popular mass-produced dolls in America. In the next decades, Chase dolls would be sold in department stores throughout New England such as Macy's, F.A.O. Schwarz, Gimbel Brothers, Best and Company, and Wanamakers. Chase made a point of offering her dolls in several sizes and in different price ranges. One of the reasons for her dolls' popularity was that they were affordable and cheaper than the more expensive French and German dolls. In the late 1890s, an average wage was between $233 and $486 a year and many of the fashion dolls sold for $5 to $25.

One of the biggest changes in doll making was the fact that Chase wanted her dolls to look more like young children than young adults. Unlike the primitive rag dolls or the more sophisticated Bisque and porcelain dolls, Chase's dolls were realistic. They had beautifully drawn and painted features that gave them a very child-like expression. Looking at the few dolls that survive, receiving a Chase doll must have been a very wonderful gift for a lucky young girl.

Izannah Walker was one of the first to claim that her dolls could be "easily kept clean." Martha Chase advertised that her dolls could be kept "germ free." Her advertisements touted the fact that her dolls were painted with insoluble paint, which was not only non-poisonous but could survive many dunkings and washings. Chase stressed that her dolls were germ-free and could be washed frequently, because her oil paint was impervious to water.

Chase later developed another source of income when she began to make a larger and more life-sized doll to be used in the training of young nurses. These Chase Hospital Dolls allowed nurses to practice on the dolls without sacrificing the comfort of real patients.

During the late 1880s, parents were becoming more health conscious and fearful of germs. And the label "sanitary toy" became a great selling point. Durability and practicality appealed to the consumer. A new line of doll companies sprung up in both the United States and England advertising sanitary, hygienic dolls that could survive heavy, daily play and abuse. Dean's Rag book dolls in England is just one example of a "hygienic doll company" product.

The fact that dolls could now be manufactured cheaply and endure heavy use appealed to business. The fact that these dolls were also washable also added to their appeal and became a major point in their promotion. Soon more and more companies were producing these dolls and finding that they were a very popular item. And since they were printed or stamped on cloth and arrived uncut, they could be sold for as little as a few cents. Most of the early cloth advertising dolls cost the consumer only 2 cents in stamps to cover handling, making their price only a fraction of the $5 to $25 price of a store-bought doll.

The mass production of cloth dolls made dolls very affordable playthings and before long more and more of the early advertising agencies sold clients on the potential of these dolls. Not only would these dolls be an inexpensive marketing tool but an effective one and soon companies were producing cheap cloth dolls to promote their products. The early cloth advertising dolls copied the popular dolls of the day in style and dress. Cloth would remain a popular medium for advertising dolls until the 1970s, when combinations of vinyl, cloth and plush would become more popular. As early as the 1900's, some businesses were creating composition dolls. Among the early examples of companies experimenting with other materials are Nabisco's Uneeda Kid, Lee's Buddy Lees, and Campbell's Campbell Kids.

After World War II there was a rush to rubber and plastic and, in the 1950s, Campbell's had an ill-fated experiment with a rubber-like substance called "magic skin," a material that was supposed to feel like human skin. Unfortunately the material aged poorly and most surviving examples of magic skin are pock marked and mottled. Later vinyl and plush velour would become popular doll materials.

Dolls would remain baby faced or look like young adolescents through the 1930s, when advertisers began to choose an older image such as Little Crow Foods Coco Wheat Gretchen, the Birdseye Merry, and the Morton Salt Girl. Unlike the earlier dolls, these were dressed in pinafores and play clothes.

Clothes and fashions have always been a selling point for doll lovers and the early advertising dolls were beautifully dressed. Miss Flaked Rice is an excellent example of an advertising doll that looks very similar to the early Chase dolls. The Singer doll is another example of the amount of attention spent to create an authentic costume look. Many of the early advertising dolls such as Dolly Dimple, Flossie Collingbourne, Miss Flaked Rice, and Trena were dressed in dainty little outfits that were modeled after popular cloth lithographed dolls of their time.

After World War II, it seemed as if young girls were impatient to grow up and dolls reflected this attitude. Dolls began to develop breasts and assume more adult female characteristics. The Ideal Novelty and Toy Company was one of the first to change its marketing strategy. In the late 1940s and 1950s, the company began to produce dolls such as the Miss Revlons, paving the way for the doll that has become a child's dream of fashion, the small-waisted, full-breasted Barbie.

The composition and hard plastic dolls of the 1940s and 1950s became more like little women. They wore makeup and adult party clothes. By the 1950s, the Revlon dolls had brought the doll industry full circle, returning to the European fashion dolls of the nineteenth century when elegant costumes became an important element in selling the doll.

Ironically, economics would once again play a role in the cloth doll industry in the 1960s when companies could no longer afford to produce dolls with finely painted facial features and elaborate costumes. Cost control dictated that production be streamlined. Beginning in the 1960s and 1970s, the new cloth Chase dolls, this time made by the Chase Bag Company of North Carolina, would create another revolution in the doll world. Chase dolls had stylized facial features — a quick curve for a mouth, a circle for a nose or an eye, a yarn mop for the hair. While early advertising dolls were being produced in the tens of thousands, by the 1970s, the concept had gone big time and advertising dolls such as Ronald McDonald and the Pillsbury Doughboy were being manufactured in the millions. And once again, it would be cost that would become the final arbiter of style.

A doll made from crepe paper and decorated with fur trim. ($10)

This doll was found in a country antique shop in Berks County, Pennsylvania. Its head is made from a dried apple. ($75)

Straw dolls from America and Japan. ($25)

This is an example of Japanese ingenuity. The doll is made of handmade Japanese papers. ($30)

Japanese Daruma dolls come in many sizes. Tradition says that when the owner gets his or her wish, the blank eye is colored in and then the doll must be destroyed in order not to appear too boastful. ($25-75)

Other styles of Japanese dolls.

Wooden Japanese dolls ($35-80)

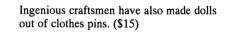

Ingenious craftsmen have also made dolls out of clothes pins. ($15)

These knitted dolls are from Scotland. ($25)

This doll was made from a corn husk. ($15)

This doll was made by a famous Thai doll-maker out of cloth. ($20)

A Romanian wine company, Trakia, offered these dolls in American in 1987 in wine stores for $4.95 and one bottle label ($10). Notice that the legs are attached to the body by wires.

This is a female Thai doll ($25). Notice her dark skin.

Johnny Gruelle registered Raggedy Ann in 1915 as a trademark and began to make dolls. ($35)

Authentic Raggedy Anns have a candy heart on their chest with the words "I Love You."

A 1920s Raggedy Ann. Note that her clothes are made of bits of older fabrics. ($150)

Two homemade Raggedy Ann and Andy dolls made without attention to details.

A homemade Orphan Annie. This character has been popular since the introduction of the comic strip Orphan Annie in the 1930s. ($50)

A painted rag doll from a private collection. Notice her mitten hands and her elaborate costume.

Levi Strauss boy dolls ($10-25)

Levi Strauss girl dolls ($10-25 depending on size and condition)

The Chicken of the Sea Mermaid ($25)

The Swiss Miss girl ($25)

Cloth dolls revolutionized the doll market and made dolls available to the average child. "Dolly Dear" was made in the 1930s by the Saalfield Publishing Company of Akron, Ohio. Dolly was printed on a sheet measuring 21 by 36 inches. She came with two doll's dolls and sold for 25 cents. She wears a stamped set of underdrawers. Young girls loved to make or buy more outfits for their dolls. ($100)

This smaller version of Dolly Dear has one of her original outfits — a lace pinafore. Dolly looks like she is five or six years old and makes a nice companion and secret friend. ($50)

This lithographed doll dates from the early part of the century. Like many dolls of this period, she has an oil-paint face and is made of patterned fabric. Her pinafore apron matches her bonnet. Her body is printed in the same matching material. ($125)

An Izannah Walker doll from a private collection. ($15,000 and up depending on condition).

This modern English scent doll has potpourri inside her skirt. ($20)

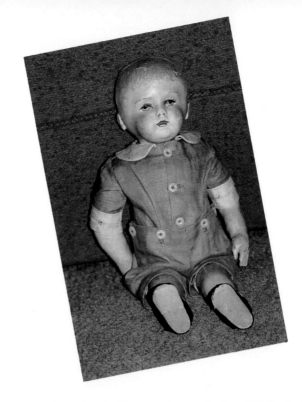

A Martha Chase boy doll from a private collection. ($1000 plus)

A Martha Jenks Chase Baby doll. It is hard to believe that this doll is really made out of cloth and that her face is painted oilskin. Chase dolls were popular because they were so realistic and child-like. ($1,000 plus)

A Heinrich Handwerck doll. Chase dolls were competing with dolls like this one, which came dressed in the height of fashion, complete with elegant headdresses, hats, feathers, and leather shoes.($1,700 plus)

An Armand Marseille child doll. This doll is 29 inches tall, the size of a young child. ($950)

An Armand Marseille Queen Louise doll. This doll is 26 inches tall. ($1,000)

Notice that this doll's head is marked with the name of the doll maker and bears the name Queen Louise. German and French doll makers would buy the heads from a craftsman who specialized in making doll heads. The custom of marking dolls continued in this country. Most cloth dolls bore the name of either their manufacturer or the product that they endorsed. With the advent of composition, hard plastic, and vinyl bodies, later hard plastic and vinyl advertising dolls would bear the name of the product stamped on the back of their heads, their necks, or somewhere else on their bodies. Good examples are the Horsman Campbell Kids, the Ideal Betsy McCall, the Gerber baby, and most of the later vinyl dolls.

These Lenci dolls were made in Italy in the 1920s and represent some of the finest cloth dolls of the day. The young girl is known as an Amori doll because of the name on her hat box. ($750 plus)

A Kammer & Reinhardt doll with flirty eyes and a wonderful pink satin dress. This doll is 25 inches tall. ($2,700 plus)

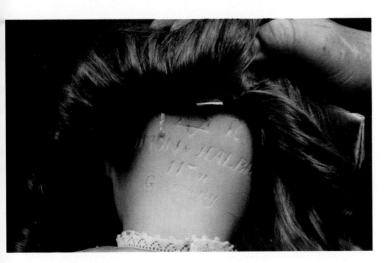

Notice that this doll is marked with the name Simon & Halbig, the shop that made the head. In addition, Kammer & Reinhardt marked their dolls with the initial K & R and a Star of David.

The label "sanitary toy" was a big selling point. This doll is one of Dean's Rag Book dolls. Notice the similarity in costume between this doll and Dolly Dimple. These dolls would come on sheets stamped with one-piece bodies and attached arms and legs. Like Dolly, these dolls would look like a typical toddler. ($100)

Miss Flaked Rice dates from 1899. She advertised Flaked Rice cereals. Notice the similarity between her face and the Chase doll. ($250)

Close up detail of Miss Flaked Rice's face.

A modern (1980s) cloth doll manufactured by Avon. This doll has stamped features reminiscent of the older style of dolls. ($15)

Chapter 2

Workers and Servants
Give the First
Product Guarantee

The cloth doll revolution had shown that consumers wanted dolls that could be played with and Martha Chase proved that dolls could be mass produced reasonably and sold at popular prices. It didn't take long for other companies to capitalize on this trend and incorporate the new lithography process to print out sheets of dolls to be sewn and assembled at home. These were given out as advertising for their products.

Like many of the store-bought cloth dolls, these early advertising dolls wore stamped and printed outfits and had very delicate facial features. The Miss Flaked Rice doll is one of the most elaborate dolls. Instructions even call for gussets and darts in the sewing of her body.

But while child dolls were the vogue for playthings, in the 1920s and 1930s companies began to create older character dolls such as Aunt Jemima, Mammy Castoria, Rastus, Anty Drudge, and Lena to promote the reliability of their product. These dolls resembled the old family housekeeper or grandmother, women competent in household skills who knew how to clean and cook. In addition these dolls carried the product in their hands or in their pockets as a subliminal message, a guarantee that these products were trustworthy and used by people who excelled at domestic tasks.

Many of these early dolls such as Aunt Jemima, Uncle Mose, Rastus, and Mammy Castoria were African-American. Doll makers had been producing such dolls since the 1800s. The early dolls, unlike the later cloth models, seldom had African-American features but were generally white dolls painted brown or black with white facial features. These dolls have always been collectibles, but with the advent of the Civil Rights Movement and the increasing Black Pride and Black Studies movements, this collectible market has gone sky high and today these dolls have become very expensive.

Most of these early dolls were sold uncut, requiring some simple sewing. Made of a lithograph-printed cloth, they were designed in one piece and all their accessories such as aprons, hats and shoes were stamped on the fabric. Most were made from linen, muslin, or art cloth. Two of the biggest manufacturers of these dolls at the turn of the century were the Arnold Print Works of Massachusetts and the Art Fabric Mills of New York. Two other companies were the Grinnell Lithographic Company of New York City and the Niagara Lithography Company of Buffalo. Grinnell

redesigned the Aunt Jemima Doll series in 1924 and Niagara manufactured the early cloth Sunny Jim Doll used by Force cereal. Many of these early cloth dolls were represented on their product's package and advertising. Like the early Chase cloth dolls, the popular Lenci dolls, and the lithographed dolls, a lot of attention was paid to the dolls' details. Notice the tiny 'O's on the Lena doll and the recurring Fels Naphtha logo on the skirt of the Anty Drudge doll. Even Aunt Jemima and her family are dressed with an eye to style. Little Wade and little Diana wear sweet play outfits and Aunt Jemima always wears a crisp, stylish, and efficient apron. Notice the little white rabbits in the corners of her apron in the 1929 version. Rastus, the Cream of Wheat man, came with his own accessories, an apron and a chef hat.

The image of Lena was used first as a trademark on the package of Blue Ribbon Malt Extract as early as 1917. The woman who was the inspiration for Lena, a robust Germanic figure, worked for the company in their test kitchen. Her age and her hardy image seemed right to represent the company. The doll, which was made pre-1930, has a sharply defined widow's peak and wears a long, green dress covered with a pattern of yellow 'O's. She holds a can of Malt Extract. Her name, Lena, can be found in one corner of her apron. Look at her shoes, they are of an unusual, three-dimensional design.

Aunt Jemima, while not one of the earliest advertising dolls, has become one of the best known. The trademark of an older, black cook, Aunt Jemima, dates to the 1880s. The idea for Aunt Jemima came about when the owner of the original pancake flour recipe saw a minstrel on the Mississippi River perform a cake-walk song and dance about a southern cook named Aunt Jemima. In 1893, the company decided to market their pancake flour with a trademark of an old black cook.

Soon the company decided to hire a 59-year-old black actress, Nancy Green, to portray Aunt Jemima in public. Green made her debut at the 1893 World's Fair in Chicago and continued to play the role for the next thirty years. In fact, Green created an entire Aunt Jemima folklore glamorizing Aunt Jemima's life. In 1923, Green died at the age of 89 years when she was hit by a car.

In 1933 another black actress, Anna Robinson, was hired to represent Aunt Jemima at the Century of Progress

Exposition in Chicago. Robinson continued to represent Aunt Jemima in public appearances until 1951. Aylene Lewis replaced Robinson and hosted the Aunt Jemima kitchen at Disneyland. Rosie Hall was the last one to portray the famous pancake maker. She gave demonstrations at state fairs until her death in 1967.

In 1905 the company printed its first paper cut-out doll. In 1908 they produced the first rag doll. From 1923 through 1945, the company produced many models of the Aunt Jemima doll, each time modernizing her image.

From 1923 through 1945, the company, which was acquired by Quaker Oats in 1925, produced a series of cloth dolls representing Aunt Jemima's family, her husband, Uncle Mose, her son, Wade, and her daughter, Diana. In the 1920s and 1930s, the Aunt Jemima dolls got another new look. By the end of the 1950s, Uncle Mose, Wade, and Diana had been dropped.

The Cream of Wheat man, Rastus, was one of the most popular and enduring images. He is dressed to resemble a waiter on a railroad Pullman car. Not only does he recall those long lost days of railroad travel, but his face has been smiling from the Cream of Wheat packages since 1899. The original trademark was based on a black waiter in a Chicago restaurant who waited on the original founders of the company.

There are two versions of the Rastus doll. The first wore black and white striped pants, the other versions came out with red and white striped pants and brown and white striped pants. The early one cost ten cents in coin and stamps when new and now sells for $150 plus. The Cream of Wheat Man came in three sizes — 16, 18, and 20 inches high. While the later one has two separate legs, some of the ear-lier ones have a one-piece leg. Many famous artists have painted the Cream of Wheat man, including James Montgomery Flagg. Rastus was also considered an arbiter of good nutrition. In 1950, the Cream of Wheat Company sent a letter along with each Rastus doll stating that hot-cooked cereals made better students.

"You know that school authorities have found by actual test that a child who eats a Hot Cooked Cereal Breakfast does a better morning's work."

The letter also offers a free booklet to parents on "The Important Business of Feeding Children." The letter ends with the hope that "Rastus will mean many happy play hours for the children."

Through the years, Rastus the Cream of Wheat Chef gained a sleeker younger look. Today he is considerably more modern than he was when he was first created.

Early advertisements for Fels Naphtha in the 1920s used a cloth Ragsy Kewpie doll named Arabella. In 1933 the company introduced the older-appearing Anty Drudge doll. Anty was intended to look like a seasoned and trustworthy cleaning woman. She wore a green apron and held a bar of Fels Naphtha soap in one hand.

Mammy Castoria first began to advertise Fletcher's Castoria in the 1930s. Like Anty Drudge, she wears an apron and holds a sample of the product. Fletcher's Castoria was a product of Glenbrook Laboratories. Mammy Castoria can be dated by the container in her hand. Prior to 1932, the Castoria bottle was packaged in a wrapper. The Castoria oil formula was patented by a Dr. Samuel Putcher, who practiced medicine in Hyannis, Massachusetts. Putcher had invented a laxative that he had been prescribing for his own patients since 1868.

A doll meant to represent African Americans has fuzzy yellow hair and blue eyes. While this doll came without any clothes, most of these dolls wear work or farm clothes. ($50)

Notice the similarity with an early "white" cloth doll. ($45)

An early black "bottle doll" from a private collection, used to cover bottles.

The most sought-after black dolls are the ones with a Mammy look. These colorfully dressed dolls with their exotic full skirts and head dresses are coveted by many white and African-American collectors who like their folk quality. ($25)

A doll from the Fiji Islands. This doll seems to have Caucasian features. ($10)

A Jamaican doll. ($15)

A floppy mop doll made in the American south. ($10)

A Brazilian topsy turvy doll. There are many theories about these topsy turvy dolls. Some say that they have religious overtones symbolizing the dual natures of mankind. Others say that black children could hide the fact that they were playing with a white doll. This doll comes from Rio de Janeiro and seems to be both a simple native mammy by day and a seductive temptress by night. Her dress is intentionally transparent. ($25)

A wooden doll from the Dominican Republic. ($10)

Notice the strange glass eyes on this felt doll. ($100) Early African-American dolls had idealized features but, beginning in the 1920s and 1930s, there seemed to be a tendency to exaggerate their features. In vaudeville, performers appeared in black face with oversized white mouths as did the Mummers in the Philadelphia New Year's parade. Later doll makers such as Norah Wellings would specialize in "island dolls" with exaggerated features and gleaming white smiles.

It is believed that the first Rastus doll was made in 1922. Another doll was introduced in 1930. The most recent doll was introduced on November 30, 1949, ($200) and is 18 inches tall and wears red and white striped pants. It is a moot point whether or not the original dolls came with detachable hats and aprons since few have survived with both the hat and apron intact.

The 11-inch Anty Drudge doll ($150) was first introduced in 1933. She holds a bar of Fels Naptha soap in one hand. ($150)

Notice that the letters of the products' name, Fels Naptha, were made into a patterned logo for her skirt.

Mammy Castoria first advertised Fletcher's Castoria in the 1930s. She can be dated by the container in her hand: prior to 1932, the Castoria bottle was packaged in a wrapper. ($150)

Lena ($95) was first used as the trademark of Blue Ribbon Malt Extract in 1917. She was modeled after one of the kitchen technicians because her Germanic face and image seemed right to represent the company. This doll was made sometime pre 1930. ($150)

Notice the care and details in the design of her outfit.

Like many dolls of this period, Lena and Anty Drudge carry products to show that they use them. Later companies would turn product endorsements into a multi-million dollar industry for celebrity endorsers.

Lena will forever carry this detailed bottle of malt extract.

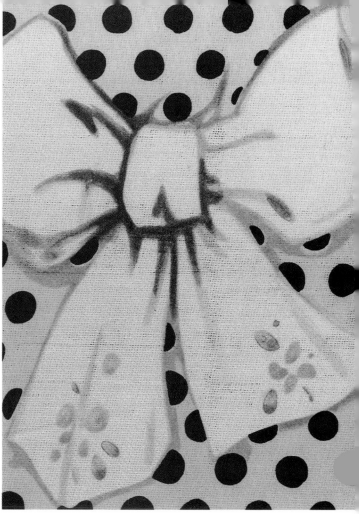

A detail from Aunt Jemima's apron.

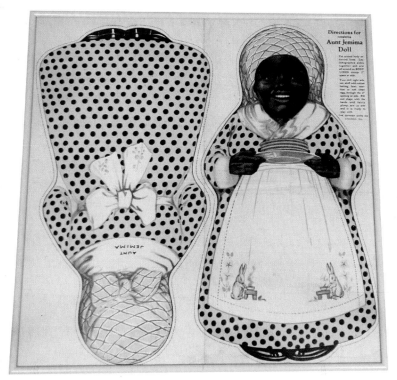

The Aunt Jemima Flour Company advertised a set of four dolls in 1919: Aunt Jemima ($150), her husband Mose ($150), and her two children, Wade and Diana ($100). Gradually the faces and figures became more refined and attractive.

Aunt Jemima and her family were always well dressed. She would never wear a plain white apron.

The company offered a set of Aunt Jemima, Uncle Mose, and their two children, Wade and Diana, made out of oilskin in 1949. These dolls are caricatures of an African-American look compared to the more attractive and realistic early versions. ($300 for the group)

A modern black advertising doll for Northern Toilet Paper was offered in 1993. ($20)

Uncle Mose ($150)

A 1923 cloth Wade ($100)

Chapter 3

Early Dolls Become Childhood Friends

Historically companies have found that children's faces strike a responsive note among adults and are therefore very effective advertising tools. In fact, in the early twentieth century, children would routinely appear in the advertising of both beer and tobacco companies even though there was no intent to suggest that children use these products.

Companies not only thought that children made good trademark images, they also thought that childlike cartoon images had greater marketing appeal to children who in turn would influence their parents to buy a product. Since a good picture was often more effective than hundreds of words of copy, a clever image was easily identifiable and carried more sway with a wider audience.

One of the earliest advertising trademarks was the charming, monocled, bon vivant Mr. Peanut. Despite Mr. Peanut's debonair flair, his origins were decidedly more plebeian. In 1900, an Italian immigrant named Amedeo Obici opened a fruit stand in Wilkes-Barre, Pennsylvania. On a whim he invested $4.50 in a peanut roaster and began to sell roasted peanuts. By 1905 the peanuts were so successful he abandoned the fruits and focused on the peanuts and, with his brother-in-law, established the Planters Nut and Chocolate Company. He chose the name Planters because it sounded more upper-class.

Obici decided to create a trademark for his peanuts in 1916 and organized a drawing contest. A 14-year-old schoolboy submitted the winning sketch of a personable gentleman peanut. Obici gave the sketch to a commercial artist to be polished. It was this unknown artist who gave Mr. Peanut a more debonair and worldly air by adding a cane, a top hat and a monocle. In 1917, Obici took out a full-page advertisement in the Saturday Evening Post and introduced Mr. Peanut to America.

One of the first Mr. Peanut dolls was made out of wood and was very popular throughout the 1930s. Since then Mr. Peanut has appeared in many forms including dolls, banks, and salt and pepper shakers. The first cloth Mr. Peanut doll was made in 1967 by the Chase Bag Company in North Carolina. By the end of this offer, more than 450,000 dolls had been sold. A second, shorter and plumper cloth Mr. Peanut doll was offered by Chase in the 1970s.

Other American companies created their own trademarks that became popular childhood playmates. Among the earliest were the Campbell Twins, the Uneeda Biscuit Boy, Cracker Jack, Sunny Jim, Buster Brown, and Philip Morris's Johnny.

The Nabisco Uneeda Kid was one of the earliest dolls and became the trademark of the Nabisco Uneeda Biscuit package. Nabisco was the trade name for the National Biscuit Company, which was founded in the 1890s by a lawyer named Adolphus Green who bought several biscuit companies in order to combine them and create a new biscuit that would have consistent good taste and shape. A savvy marketer, Green hired an advertising agency to develop a catchy slogan and create a new brand name. In 1898, after a long search, he settled on the name "Uneeda" because he liked its classic, magical sound.

In 1900, the company decided to create a trademark for its Uneeda advertising campaign. One of the agency's copywriters asked his 5-year-old nephew, Gordon Still to pose for an advertising photographer. Still wore a yellow slicker and boots and carried a box of Uneeda Biscuits. The agency liked the image of the little boy so much that they modified it and created the Uneeda Kid. The first Uneeda Kid was manufactured in 1914 by the Ideal Novelty and Toy Company from a design made by Morris Mictom, founder of the Ideal Toy Company.

Another childhood favorite was Buster Brown and his dog Tige. The pair was created as cartoon characters by Richard Outcault in May 1904. The comic strip ran regularly in the Sunday New York Herald and thousands of children followed the adventures of Buster Brown and his dog Tige. After a while Outcault founded his own advertising company to market Buster Brown and eventually sold the use of the name to more than forty-five companies, of which two, Buster Brown Shoes and Buster Brown Hosiery, used the image of the young boy and his dog as advertising dolls.

Through the years advertising dolls reflected the fashions of the day which, until the late 1940s and early 1950s, showed well-dressed young girls and boys. But after World War II, formality gave way to informality and dolls, like the young children of the day, assumed a more informal way of dress.

One of the first companies to use the image of an all-American boy-and-girl look was the Birdseye Company, which created a trio of very likable children — Minx, Merry, and Mike. Unlike the cherubic Campbell Twins, the Birdseye trio look mischievous and ready for play. At one point the three jolly twins were considered among the country's top-four most recognizable trademarks. Borden's Elsie the Cow, Aunt Jemima, and the Campbell Kids were the others. The Birdseye triplets popularized the products of the company whose name derives from the company's founder, Clarence Bob Birdseye, the inventor of frozen food. An explorer, adventurer, and inventor, Birdseye discovered, while living in Labrador with his family, that he could keep his vegetable supply frozen in a barrel of ice for months, defrosting pieces depending on need. In 1923, Birdseye received a patent for his idea. Birdseye apparently owed his name to an ancestor whose arrow pierced the eye of a hawk. Today, after only fifty-five years, the Birdseye trio is almost unknown.

Two dolls are known to have represented the Ceresota and Heckers Flour companies. The first is dated 1912, the second 1972. The early doll is 16 inches high and was printed in rich, oil-based paints. He wears dark red pants, a white, short-sleeved shirt, blue suspenders, and a brown hat. The more recent doll dates from 1972 and was made by the Chase Company and advertised on bags of flour for a dollar. Standing 15 inches high, it was printed in purple and is known as either the Ceresota doll or the Heckers doll.

Since the early 1900s, cereals have been one of the biggest promoters of trademark dolls. The early dolls were either fairy tale or historical figures such as the Quaker Oat Man, the Quaker Crackels boy, and Kellogg's Goldilocks, Tom, Tom, the Piper's son, and Little Bo Beep. Later companies created dolls that were more child-like, such as Coco Wheat Puffs' Gretchen or Quaker Puffed Rice and Wheat's Puffy. In the 1930s, Kellogg's introduced humanized animals such as Freckles the Frog, Crinkle the Cat, Dandy Duck, and Dinkey the Dog. Notice that these animals all wear human clothes and have the appearance of dapper dandies.

In the 1960s, animal dolls would have fewer anthropomorphic features and become more cartoonish, while still retaining their animal natures, such as Tony the Tiger, Sam the Froot Loops Toucan, and Dig 'Em the frog.

One of the earliest cereal advertising dolls was Sunny Jim, a pessimist whose personality was transformed after eating his Force Cereal. He first appeared as a doll in 1905. He was reissued in 1978. Few remember that Force cereal was a big contender in the American cereal market from 1905 through 1915. Today the cereal can no longer be found in the United States. A jolly, white wigged colonial gentleman, Sunny Jim has been the cereal's spokesman since 1905 when the first doll, an 18-inch muslin doll, was designed by W.W. Denslow, the same man who illustrated the original "Wizard of Oz." In 1909, the company produced another doll with a composition head and a stuffed body. Sunny Jim got his name from the slogan, "Be Bright as the Sun, Cute as can be. I'm yours 'for fun' as you can see."

The Campbell Company was founded in New Jersey in 1869 by Abram Anderson and Joseph Campbell. They originally sold only canned peas and asparagus. Campbell took over the company in 1873 and began to sell canned vegetables and fruit butters. In 1897, Dr. Joseph Dorrance developed a formula for condensed soups and the company began to sell five different varieties. The Campbell Kids were introduced as a trademark in 1904 and were first used by the company as streetcar cards and in an advertisement in Ladies' Home Journal. The kids were a brainchild of Philadelphia artist Grace Gebbie Weiderseim Drayton, who sketched them at her husband's request using herself as the model. Drayton continued to sketch the roly-poly faced Campbell Kids for the next twenty years. Originally they were just healthy looking boys and girls. Later they would be dressed as policemen, athletes, sailors, soldiers, and Colonial characters. In the late 1980s, they became multi-cultural and the Black Campbell Kid was introduced. In the early days a rhyming couplet accompanied each promotion:

"We blend the best with careful pains
In skillful combination
And every single can contains
Our business reputation."

The first Campbell's Kid doll dates back to 1909. It was made of velvet. In 1910 the Horsman Company made its first Campbell Soup Kid. The doll had a cloth body and came in four sizes and had what was described as a "can't break 'em' head. Campbell Kid dolls were first distributed in England in 1911 and the following year the company took out its first patent for the doll and began to introduce a series of Campbell dolls. In 1916, the company introduced a 16-inch tall Campbell Kid doll with cloth legs. In 1916 Sears began to sell the dolls in their catalogs. From 1954 to 1955, the company manufactured squeeze toys. Also, that year the company tried a new approach and released a set of "magic skin" chef dolls. The "magic skin," a new form of latex rubber, didn't last and became discolored. In 1956, an official birthday promotion Campbell Kid doll was introduced.

From the 1950s through the 1970s, there were many more varieties of Kids. In the 1950s, the doll was modernized and, in 1954 in celebration of their fiftieth birthday, a new Campbell Kid was introduced. There was a similar promotion in the 1960s and again in 1971. In 1963, the company sold a line of Scotch Highlander dolls and in 1966-68, a Campbell Soup chef doll. In 1973, the Japanese got into the market and manufactured a set of cloth boy and girl dolls. In 1976, a set of bicentennial Campbell Kids was introduced. These Kids were dressed in Colonial-style clothing. In 1978, the company created a larger-scaled doll and later also released an African-American version.

Probably the most famous baby face in the advertising world is the Gerber Baby. The original image was based on a half-finished charcoal sketch made in 1928 by a then-unknown artist, Dorothy Hope Smith. Since then the company has offered at least five Gerber Baby dolls as promotions. The first was introduced in 1936. It was 8 inches tall and cost 10 cents plus three product labels and came in either pink or blue. The girl baby wore a long baby dress, booties, and a bonnet with ribbon ties. She holds a can of Gerber baby food in one hand and a toy dog in the other. The boy is dressed in a blue outfit. During the three years this offer continued, approximately 27,000 dolls were sold.

In 1954, a 12-inch, rubber Gerber baby was introduced for $2.00 and twelve product labels. A rubber Gerber baby was sold in 1955 that came with baby accessories such as a cry box, a bottle, and a doll-sized cereal dish and spoon. The original mold was sculpted by Bernard Lipfert, who also created the Shirley Temple Doll. In 1972, a 10-inch, firm vinyl doll was sold for $2.50 and four product labels. It was manufactured by the Uneeda Company and had painted eyes, a rosebud mouth, and blonde hair. This was the first time Gerber offered a doll with yellow hair. An African-American Gerber baby was introduced in the same year. To celebrate its fiftieth anniversary, Gerber introduced another doll in 1978. The doll was a faithful replica of the original Smith sketch.

The idea for Cracker Jack owes its origin to a confection created in 1890 by F.W. Rueckheim, who one day dipped a handful of popcorn and peanuts into molasses syrup. One of the first people to sample this new confection announced. "That's a cracker jack," and the name stuck. The Sailor boy trademark came along after World War I, when the company wanted to look patriotic. Cracker Jack was the first company to introduce a wax-sealed, waterproof package. Another marketing twist was a small toy surprise inside each box. Initially these toys were metal. Today they are mostly plastic.

The Morton Salt trademark traces its origins back to the 1914 when the then 50-year-old company was looking for a way to advertise that its salt was free-flowing. A Boston agency, the Ayer Company, was hired and submitted ten ideas. Sterling Morton, the son of the founder, liked the one showing Ayer's own daughter with an umbrella over her head, walking in the rain carrying a can of salt under her arm. Even though it was raining, the salt was pouring out of the can. Thus the slogan, "When it Rains, It Pours," was born. Morton later said that he chose this sketch because it reminded him of his own daughter, and soon the little girl in the yellow rain slicker became known as the Morton Salt girl.

The most popular versions of these two — Cracker Jack and the Morton Salt Girl — were the 1974 Mattel Shoppin' Pals.

One of the biggest promoters of advertising premium offers has been the W.H. Kellogg Company. The first Kellogg premium was "The Funny Jungleland Moving Picture Book." It was offered in 1910 and cost 10 cents and a Kellogg's Corn Flakes box top. Between 1910 and 1912, more than 2.5 million copies of the "Funny Jungleland" book were distributed.

Kellogg promoted its first series of cloth dolls in 1926. These dolls reflected the innocence of a time when parents read fairy tales to their children, who learned to recite nursery rhymes in school. Most playtime activities centered around these fairy tales and stories about young heroines and heroes such as Heidi, Hans Brinker, and Horatio Alger. It was a time of innocence and happy endings. Early Kellogg advertising dolls borrowed popular images from Mother Goose rhymes. In 1925, Kellogg introduced its first dolls, a series of four — Goldilocks and the Three Bears. These four dolls are among the most popular for collectors today. The company offered the Fairyland series in 1928 — Tom the Piper's Son, Bo Beep, Mary and Her Little Lamb and Red Riding Hood. Uncut, they cost 30 cents and one box top from Kellogg's Corn Flakes. These dolls are harder to find.

The company introduced a set of friendly animals — Dinkey the Dog, Crinkle the Cat, Dandy the Duck and Freckles the Frog — in 1935 to promote Wheat Krispies. The dolls, which also came uncut, cost 10 cents each and one box top. For the price of 25 cents and four box tops, you could get all four. Although Snap, Crackle, and Pop were created in 1928, they didn't become dolls until 1948, when they were offered for 15 cents and a box top from Rice Krispies.

Chiquita Banana became a trademark in 1944, designed by a Chicago advertising company to go along with a jingle written for the United Fruit Company. The image of a dancing senorita came from the jingle. Chiquita was the first advertising doll to be released by two different companies. In 1944, it was offered to Kellogg's customers to promote Corn Flakes cereal. The second Chiquita doll was a squeeze toy and was sold as a bath toy in the 1950s. The third doll was offered as a mail-in premium in 1974. It was mass-produced and offered in women's magazines and the Sunday comics. The doll cost a $1.75 plus two seals from Chiquita bananas and came in a kit which included a record of the jingle. Eventually the trademark became so popular the bananas became a subsidiary of the United Fruit Company. The first Kellogg Chiquita Banana doll was of unusually poor quality and the colors faded very quickly. Chiquita was reintroduced in 1974 in another form by the Chase Bag Company to advertise Chiquita Brand Bananas. This is one of the few dolls to come as a premium from two such different companies.

In the fifties, Kellogg offered an entirely different series of vinyl dolls. Its first offer was the 1954 Sweetheart Sue, a vinyl, blonde-haired young girl who came with a bonnet and an apron. She cost one dollar and was one of several little girl dolls offered by the company throughout the 1950s and 1960s. Other dolls were Baby Ginger, a majorette doll, and Little Miss Kay. These dolls were premium offers for Sugar Frosted Flakes, Sugar Smacks, Sugar Pops, Raisin Bran, and Cocoa Krispies.

In 1950, in an offer geared to young boys, the company offered a set of three plastic U.S. Navy Frogmen.

In 1964, the company returned to cloth dolls and produced Toucan Sam and Hillbilly Goat, and in 1974 they hit the jackpot with a large, stuffed tiger named Tony and a frog named Dig 'Em. Tony the Tiger appears on the Frosted Flakes package and Dig 'Em appears as the trademark on Sugar Smacks.

In addition, the company also offered a lot of baseball memorabilia.

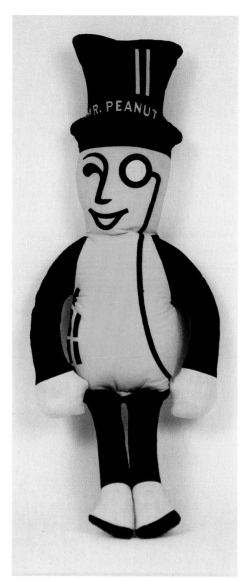

This doll was made by the Chase Bag Company in two sizes. Notice the different colorations in the body, the placement of the monocle and the shoes.

A plastic Mr. Peanut peanut grinder. ($75)

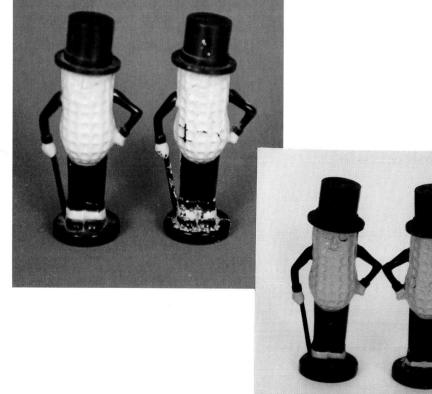

The faces on these Mr. Peanut salt and pepper shakers ($35) are almost worn off.

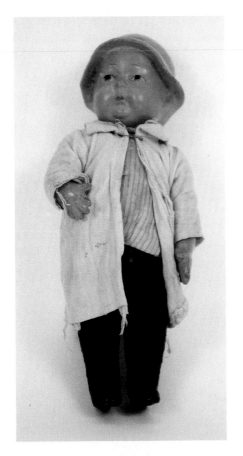

The Uneeda doll was designed in 1914 by Morris Mictom, founder of the Ideal Novelty and Toy Company. The original model for the image was five-year-old Gordon Still. ($425-450)

Buster Brown and his dog Tige ($25 each) was created as a cartoon character by Richard Outcault in 1904.

This Buster Brown doll ($25) was made in 1974.

Three lithographed cloth dolls, Merry, Minx, and Mike, were a 1953 General Foods Corporation promotional push for Birdseye frozen orange juice. At one point these three jolly children were considered among the country's top four most recognizable trademarks. Borden's Elsie the Cow, Aunt Jemina, and the Campbell Kids were the other three. What is particularly captivating about them is their mischievous lip-smacking grin. ($40 each)

An uncut, unsewn Merry. ($50)

Notice that Merry has a bow-tied pigtail.

In the 1940s and 1950s, cloth promotional dolls reflected clothes children wore at the time — girls typically wore jumpers and aprons; boys wore jeans. Children's play clothes seemed to favor a lot of plaids and check designs.

There are two versions of the Ceresota boy. ($25) An early one dated in 1912 and another from 1972. The early doll is 16 inches high and wears dark red pants, a white, short-sleeved shirt, blue suspenders, and a brown hat.

The more recent Ceresota doll was made in 1972 ($20) by the Chase Company and is dressed in purple. He is often called the Heckers Flour boy.

Few remember that Force cereal was an early twentieth century contender for the American cereal market. Sunny Jim has been company spokesman since 1905. Today the doll is only sold in England. This one is dated from 1978 and carries a replica of the original Force cereal box. Sunny Jim is one of the few advertising dolls in profile. ($25)

Vinyl squeak Campbell Kids made in the 1950s. ($45 each)

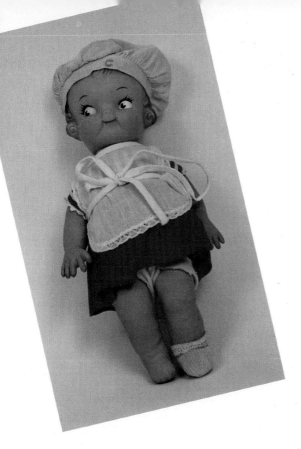

This "magic skin" Campbell's chef was made in 1955 to celebrate the 50th anniversary of the Campbell Kids. ($75 depending on condition and accessories.)

1963 Scotch Highlander doll kit ($75)

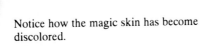

Notice how the magic skin has become discolored.

The 1973 version made by a Japanese company ($60 for the set.)

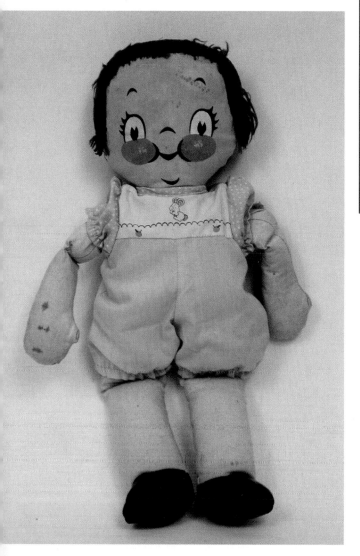

A Japanese Campbell Kid doll dressed in homemade clothes.

1976 Campbell's Bicentennial dolls ($40 each)

A 1978 large Campbell Kid ($85)

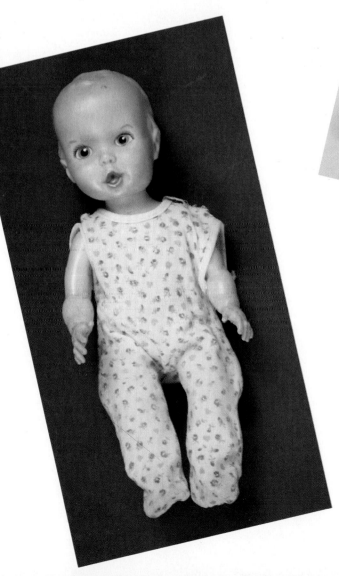

The Gerber Baby was probably the most famous baby face in the advertising world. There were many different Gerber babies. This doll dates from 1972. It is a 10-inch firm vinyl doll and was originally sold for $2.50 and four product labels. It was manufactured by the Uneeda Company and had painted eyes, a rosebud mouth, and blonde hair. This was the first time Gerber offered a doll with yellow hair. ($65)

A 1960s Campbell Soup cup ($15)

Cracker Jack the happy sailor not only gave you a good taste treat but also a toy. ($25)

Note the metal surprises on his hat. How many people remember reaching their hands down into the package, pushing away the caramelized popcorn and pulling out a small wrapped package.

A third Cracker Jack doll was made by Vogue in 1980 ($60).

Like many of the early trademark children, the Morton Salt Girl ($25) was based on a real child. Mattel manufactured this version in 1974.

Arbuckle Brothers Coffee issued four story book dolls in 1931 based on familiar nursery rhymes, this sad one being Jack with his pail, and a kerchief covering his broken crown.

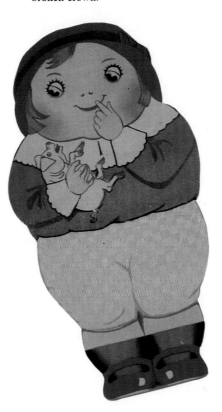

Oxol was an early laundry bleach and household cleaner. This Oxol doll ($80) was introduced in 1931 and wears the diamond-checked red, white, and blue colors of the Oxol bottle. So often these dolls, like their more elaborate composition and plastic contemporaries, reveal a lot about fashion. Note the wind-blown curly hairdo, the rouged cheeks, and the rosebud mouth.

This is Tom, the Piper's son. Others in the series included Jack's partner in the climb, Jill, and Mary with her lamb. Later Arbuckle Brothers coffee became known as Yuban.

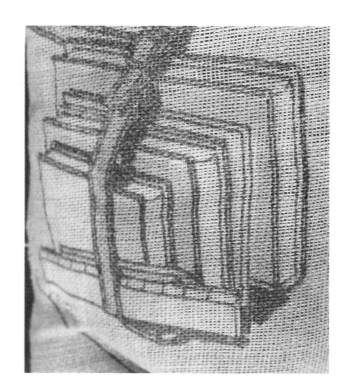

A detail of the book bag.

American Beauty Macaroni Company introduced Roni Mac in 1937. This is one of the few dolls designed in a cylinder form. He has no ears but carries a book-bag strap. Originally he was a mail-in premium and cost 25 cents and one box top. ($85)

The 1926 Goldilocks and the **Three Bear** Series ($500 for the uncut set)

The back of the doll.

Papa Bear uncut ($125)

Papa Bear cut and sewn ($100)

Detail of face.

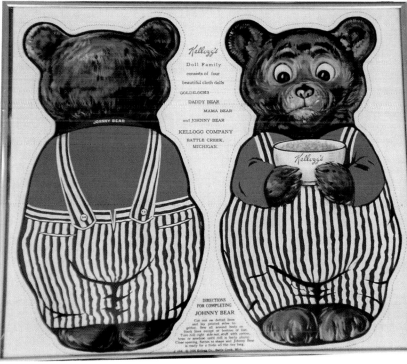

Baby Bear uncut ($125)

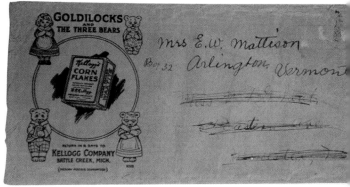

Mailing envelope.

Mama Bear uncut ($125)

54

The 1928 Fairyland Series from Kellogg's
with Little Bo Beep ($150)

The 1928 Tom the Piper's Son ($150)

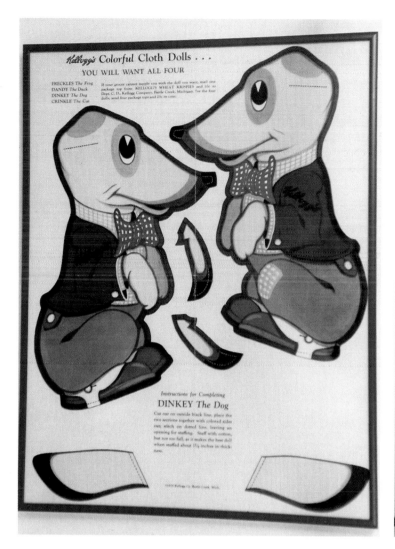

1935 Dinkey the Dog ($100)

1935 Crinkle the Cat ($100)

A sewn Crinkle cat ($90)

The back of Crinkle.

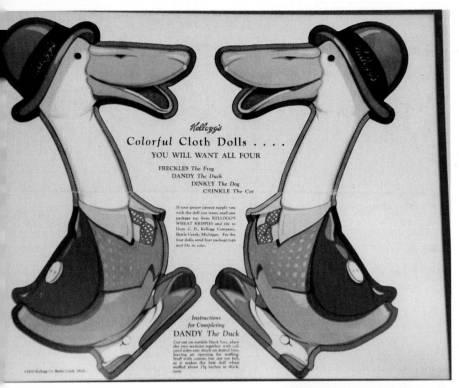

1935 Dandy the Duck ($100)

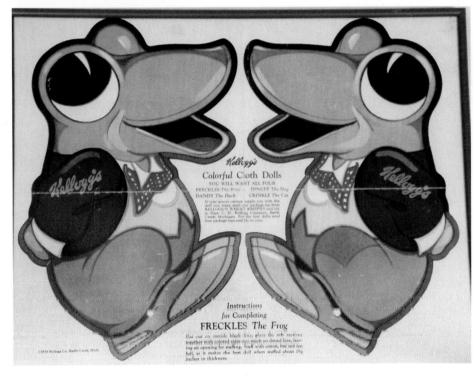

1935 Freckles the Frog

A sewn version.

These Rice Crispies' Snap, Crackle, and Pop dolls were a premium in 1948 and 1954. ($325 for the set)

1948 Snap ($100)

1954, Snap ($60)

1948 Pop ($100)

1954, Pop ($60)

A Rice Crispies' 1948 mailing envelope.

1948 Crackle ($100)

1954 Crackle mailing envelope

In 1975, Snap, Crackle, and Pop made their debut in vinyl as squeeze toys. ($35 each)

Later they were introduced in miniature. ($10 each)

Mini Snap, Crackle, and Pop ($10)

The first Chiquita Banana doll was introduced in 1949 to promote Corn Flakes. ($125)

This doll was a mail-in offer in 1974. ($35)

The mail-in coupon.

The Chiquita Banana record.

1953 Sweetheart of the Corn doll ($45)

"I'm Chiquita Banana and I've Come to Say'" became a popular jingle.

The 1953 Sweetheart of the Corn doll was made out of vinyl and had rooted blond hair.

The dolls of the 1950s came with elaborate outfits with many accessories. Compare the Sweetheart doll with the Campbells' Chef and the Bicentennial Campbell girl. (See Page 49)

The Sweetheart doll came with an extra outfit for play.

Toucan Sam ($20) was introduced in 1964 to advertise Froot Loops.

Toucan Sam in vinyl.

1969 Kellogg's mini people ($10)

1969 Drooper, a Kellogg's Banana Split doll ($50)

1970, Tony the Tiger ($35)

Tony in plush ($10), cloth ($35), and vinyl ($20)

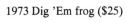

1973 Dig 'Em frog ($25)

A 1970s Kellogg's Fun Fair clown ($25)

Little Crow Foods, an Indiana food company, introduced a 10-year-old blonde with pigtails named Gretchen ($55) on its boxes of Coco Wheat Puffs from 1949 through 1965. Like many of the girl dolls of this vintage, she wears a white pinafore over a red and white checked dress.

Dig 'Em in miniature ($15)

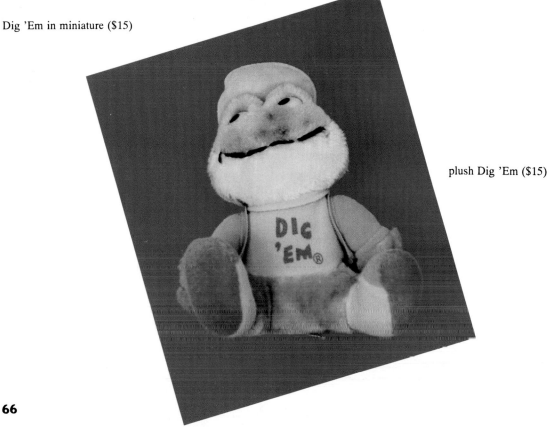

plush Dig 'Em ($15)

An unidentified cereal doll. ($25)

A group of Norah Wellings sailor dolls used to advertise ocean liners of the day. ($75 to $120)

These Norah Wellings sailor dolls were used to advertise ocean liners of the day. ($75 to $120)

This is an example of a sailor with a big smile and protruding ears.

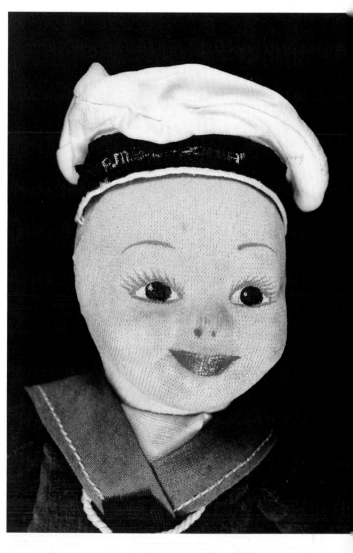

This is an example of a sailor without a smile and protruding ears.

This is an unusual sailor doll with a full head of hair.

A copy of a Wellings sailor.

This doll has a grin and protruding ears.

The authentic dolls are labeled on their feet or on their back.

Label on back

Other Wellings labels.

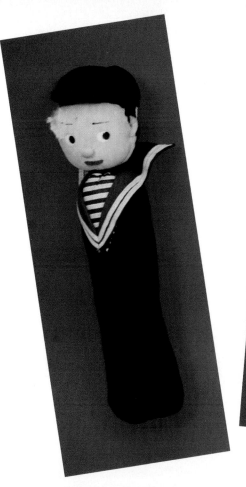

Although they are not labelled, they have a look very different from their English contemporaries.

A French bowling doll. These dolls were used on the French transatlantic liners during the 1940s and 1950s as a table game. ($100)

Compare these Wellings dolls with other felt dolls such as Lencis.

A 1967 Kuddles from the Knickerbocker Toy Company. ($65)

Chapter 4

Silly Animals and Cartoon Characters Invite Boys to Play

Although doll makers have always made boy dolls, historically doll play has been a female activity. Beginning in the twentieth century, with the popularization of the Teddy Bear and similar stuffed animals, doll play became a comfort to both boys and girls. But it wasn't until the popularization of cloth dolls and animals, that dolls would become confidantes and emotional playthings for both boys and girls. It was through these soft, cuddly cloth playmates that both boys and girls found a bedtime companion.

One of the earliest advertising boy dolls was Buddy Lee, a doll created for the H.D. Lee Company to promote their line of work uniforms. The idea for this cute Kewpie-look-a-like doll came about in 1920. The first doll was 12-1/2 inches tall, made of composition with his eyes glancing to the side. The first Buddy Lee came with two uniforms, a cowboy outfit and an engineer's suit. The dolls originally cost the dealer $13.50 a dozen. The Buddy Lee dolls were dressed in Lee clothing and intended to be used in window displays. Sold singly, they cost $2.50. The most popular early Buddy Lee dolls were the Cowboy and the Engineer.

Lee Jeans was the first company to use a zipper fly and also the first to vat-dye the jeans so that the colors wouldn't run. Lee provided uniforms for many firms including Coca-Cola, Sinclair Oil, John Deere, and T.W.A. All in all, there were more than seventeen different Buddy Lees including a 1949 plastic version.

Unlike Kellogg, General Mills seemed to aim its marketing toward boys rather than girls right from the start. In fact, General Mills seemed to steer clear of the doll market until the 1970s. With the exception of one short-lived foray in the early 1970s, when it did offer promotional dolls, the company preferred to produce silly animals or cartoon characters such as the Trix Rabbit and the fanciful BooBerry, Frankenberry, and Count Chocula.

General Mills was established in 1866 on the banks of the Mississippi River in a mill near Minneapolis, Minnesota. For the next fifteen years the company developed several brands of flour. In 1880, the company entered three brands of its flours in an international Millers Competition. The winning flour was awarded a gold medal, hence the name Gold Medal. A Gold Medal doll was issued in the 1920s.

One of the world's most famous trademarks, Betty Crocker, was created in 1921 as a pen name for the company's Consumer Response Department. In 1921, Gold Medal had offered a flour-sack pincushion to anyone completing a jigsaw puzzle of a mill scene. Many people included baking questions with their responses and the president of the company, Washburn Crosby, decided that a woman should answer these questions. Hence the mythical character of Betty Crocker was born. Her last name was a tribute to a popular retiring General Mills director, William Crocker. Her first name was chosen as a friendly sounding name. Although Betty Crocker was not a real person, she had her own radio cooking school, wrote cookbooks, gave out recipes, and, by 1945, was chosen as the second best-known woman in the United States according to a Fortune Magazine survey. Eleanor Roosevelt was number one. Through the years, Betty Crocker has undergone many facial remakes. A Betty Crocker doll was produced in the 1950s.

General Mills' first cereal, Wheaties, was introduced in 1924, Bisquick in 1928, and Cheerios in 1941. Wheaties was the first ready-to-eat wheat cereal; Cheerios the first ready to eat oat cereal. Count Chocula (1971) was the first chocolate-flavored cereal. Boo Berry (1973) was the first with blueberry flavor.

Wheaties first touted itself as "the breakfast of champions" in 1933 and from then on enlisted the aid of famous athletes to promote it. Their initial thrust was in the world of baseball. Stars such as Babe Ruth, Joe DiMaggio, Stan Musial, Phil Rizzuto, Jackie Robinson, Ted Williams, Hank Greenberg, Roy Campanella, Pee Wee Reese, and Yogi Berra have endorsed the product.

Wheaties became the first company to commercially sponsor a televised sports broadcast — the August 29, 1939, baseball game between the Cincinnati Reds and the Brooklyn Dodgers — for some five hundred television owners in New York City. While Cheerios and Wheaties never had a doll promotion associated with their packages, both had very successful ad and premium campaigns.

In 1932, Wheaties became one of the first cereals to turn to radio when they introduced a young boy character named Skippy, who would plug the cereal to the kids. Wheaties' sponsorship of Skippy lasted until 1933, when the two parted company.

In that same year a new character was born — Jack Armstrong, the all-American boy. With the advent of this new radio adventure show, Wheaties not only enlarged its audience appeal but began to issue a long-running series of Jack Armstrong premiums. Jack Armstrong Explorer Telescopes and Sky Ranger model planes helped promote Wheaties' sales. In 1951, Jack Armstrong left the airwaves and Wheaties returned to its sports endorsements in 1957, after a brief but disappointing fling with cartoon characters.

While General Mills created many trademark figures that strike nostalgic notes for us all, they seldom transferred these images into a doll. Among their most famous besides Betty Crocker was Wheaties' Jack Armstrong, the all American boy. General Mills was one of the first companies to recognize the importance of radio, and later television, and preferred the broadcasting route to using print trademarks.

Cheerios also tried to create cartoon characters for radio and print. In 1942, Cheerios introduced Cheeri O'Leary, an animated figure who gave out biographical information about movie stars of the day. In 1944, the company introduced Joe Idea, an animated figure who always thinks of Cheerios. And from 1953 through 1972 there were more characters, the Cheerios Kid and Sue and, in 1977, there was a stick figure cartoon character Cheeriodle who promoted Cheerios through the 1980s.

Both Wheaties and Cheerios seemed to focus on appealing to young men. While Wheaties focused on sports and fitness, Cheerios tried to appeal to the adventure-loving nature of a young boy, starting its premium campaign in 1940 with items used by popular pop-culture action figures. One of their longest relationships was with the Lone Ranger. In 1941 the cereal gave out Lone Ranger Defender Silver Bullets and a Flashlight pistol. In 1944, it was a Lone Ranger decoder, and in 1945 a Lone Ranger pedometer. The affiliation with the Lone Ranger lasted through 1961. From then on, Cheerios looked to cartoon characters such as Bullwinkle, Bugs Bunny, Mickey Mouse, and subjects from Hanna-Barbera cartoons. The Lone Ranger was resurrected in 1981 with the offer of a Deputy Kit, but his return was short-lived. The company returned to adventure and action, offering premiums from the world of race cars and Star Trek.

For many years, General Mills seemed to have avoided the doll market, but in the 1970s they too got on the doll band wagon. However, their first dolls did not have any cereal identification. In 1971, the company offered a 6-1/2 inch Dawn doll for three Cheerio box tops or 75 cents with one box top. In 1972 the company offered two more vinyl 6-1/2 inch dolls, Sippin' Sam and Sippin' Sue. Both dolls were dressed in western garb. But in 1975, recognizing the importance of product identification, the company issued a set of 7- to 8-inch, molded vinyl monster dolls Boo Berry, Fruit Brute, Frankenberry, and Count Chocula. They cost $1 plus a box top of their namesake cereal.

In 1977 the company issued its most popular doll, the Trix Rabbit. The idea for a silly rabbit who prefers cereal to carrots was born in 1960, six years after the cereal had been in the marketplace. For the next thirty years, Trix would have a series of adventures as he tries to finish his bowl of cereal.

The Crackels doll from Quaker is thought to date from 1924 through 1930. The cereal was short-lived and never achieved the popularity of other Quaker Oats brands such as Puffed Wheat and Puffed Rice.

The Quaker Oats brand name has been in existence since the 1850s. The company's founder, Henry Seymour, chose the name Quaker because he was impressed by the Quakers' purity and honor. His partner, William Heston, agreed with this idea and, inspired by a picture of William Penn, helped design the Quaker Oats Man. Through the years the Quaker Oats Man has become more and more robust than his earlier image.

Quaker Oats has been one of the leaders in promoting premium dolls. Their most famous was Aunt Jemima. The Quaker Oats Company purchased the Aunt Jemima Pancake Flour Company in 1926 and introduced its first doll offer, a set of four cloth dolls, in 1928. The dolls sold for 25 cents each. Another coveted Quaker Oats collectible was the Puffy soldier figure introduced in 1930. In the 1960s, Quaker offered another doll, a bumbling sea captain, Cap'n Crunch. This doll promoted the company's first sweetened cereal. It cost more than $5 million for the company to introduce this new brand of cereal and within two years it was considered one of the country's most popular sweetened cereals. In 1978, the company issued a fabric Cap'n Crunch based on the historical pirate Jean Lafitte. In 1989, another Cap'n Crunch was introduced. Later, two more cloth dolls, a Quake doll and a Quisp doll were introduced for Quake and Quisp cereals.

One of the most famous felt cloth doll makers was Englishwoman Norah Wellings. Wellings' dolls, especially her ocean liner dolls, became popular souvenirs of the great ocean liners of the 1930s through the 1950s. These dolls were sold on board ship and in shore shops. The sailors come in two styles, a grinning sailor with protruding ears and pointed feet and a smiling sailor with velvet feet and flat ears. In addition to sailors, Wellings created soldiers, airmen, and exotic South Sea islanders. Wellings opened her first factory in Stropshire, England, in 1926. Her dolls are made of soft velvet and are marked either on the foot, back, or wrist with a black, blue, or beige label.

Other early trademarks were associated with the automotive and trucking industry. The idea for a bulldog mascot representing Mack Trucks came about during World War I when the British troops would refer to these hardy American trucks as "bulldogs." The early Mack AC trucks with their snub-nosed hoods resembled a bulldog and the tenacity with which they moved through mud and muck to serve the American and British troops in the trenches reinforced the image. In 1922, the bulldog became the official company mascot.

In 1933, a Mack engineer, A.F. Masury, entered a soap-carving contest with a cubist rendering of a bulldog. The company took that model as the company's hood ornament, and the image stuck. A bull dog has adorned the hoods of Mack trucks ever since.

Another automotive image which has become a world-wide symbol is the Michelin man. Originally the Michelin brothers, Andre and Edouard, patented an air-filled tire with an innertube that could be easily repaired by removing it from its rim. Previously vehicles used solid tires with tubes glued into them. The Michelin tires became an instant success and a favorite of French bicycle riders. Around the turn of the century while touring a exhibition in Lyons, the Michelin brothers spotted a display of tires stacked one on top of the other. Said Edouard, "Just add arms and you've got a man." Four years later the Michelins hired French poster artist O'Galop to refine the image and the Michelin man, Bibendum, was born. The French name "Bibendum" came from the Michelin slogan that their tires could swallow up obstacles.

Companies also turned to animal spokesmen. One of the most popular animal personalities has been the talking fish, Charlie the tuna. Whoever dumped the yellow-slickered fisherman pictured on the Star-Kist Tuna can for a smart-aleck, fast-talking blue tuna named Charlie was a genius. Charlie, with his beret and sunglasses and street-wise charm, has become one of the most charming and lovable advertising characters around. Originally Charlie was drawn with shark teeth and a ferocious look, but his appearance was softened and he was given a voice by former Yiddish actor Herschel Bernardi, better known for his starring role as Tevye in "Fiddler on the Roof." Before long Charlie became Mr. Personality of the advertising world and a favorite among consumers, who never tired of hearing about the struggles of the tuna who wanted to be a Star-Kist tuna with good taste.

Charlie was first promoted as a pillow doll in 1969 and in 1970 by Mattel. He talked and had nine responses including "Have you ever heard of a talking tuna before?" and the famous "Sorry Charlie." A Charlie-the-tuna bathroom scale was first advertised in "Good Housekeeping" in July 1972: "For only $5.95 and 3 Star-Kist labels here's something that makes watching your weight fun." Since then he has been offered in the form of a telephone, a bank, and a lamp and has been manufactured in cloth, plush, and vinyl. Through the years Charlie still struggles for acceptance and perhaps it is this underdog aspect that has made this talking fish so lovable.

Another animal spokesman was Smokey the Bear, who became a symbol for forest-fire prevention in 1944. His image was designed by Albert Stahl of the Foote, Cone, and Belding agency. But the bear wasn't officially used by the United States Department of Agriculture, Forest Service until 1947.

Many books have been written about Smokey. The Smokey Bear Campaign was one of the first environmental awareness campaigns conducted in the United States. Smokey made Americans aware of the horrors of forest fires and the dangers of playing with matches. The campaign began in 1946 when the U.S. Forest Service decided to adopt a spokesman bear. A real life Smokey bear became a national figure in 1950 when a little bear cub was found with his burned paws clinging to a charred tree branch, the only survivor of a New Mexico forest fire. The wounded bear was brought to Washington, D.C., where he became the living embodiment of the symbolic representative of the U.S. Forest Service. For many years Smokey was the star of all U.S. Forest Service advertisements and even had his own zip code. At the height of his popularity, he was receiving more than 13,000 letters a week.

Smokey the Bear as an advertising premium was first introduced in 1976 by Aim Toothpaste. That was the year that the live Smokey bear died.

In the 1960s, the U.S. Department of Agriculture introduced Woodsy Owl, who wanted America to "Give a Hoot, Don't Pollute." Woodsy became the spokesman for a national anti-litter campaign.

The Coca Cola patent dates to the 1880s when a Georgia pharmacist concocted a new headache remedy, but it wasn't until the 1930s when the company began a series of promotional offers. Although its most famous doll was the Coca Cola Santa, its first known doll was the 1930 Tickletoes the Wonder Doll. The next doll was a Buddy Lee doll dressed as a Coca-Cola route salesman. In 1958, a Santa Claus was introduced. Santa had been associated with the company since the Great Depression when artist Haddon Sundblom was hired to draw a Santa. Haddon decided to soften the traditionally severe look of St. Nicholas and, using a retired Coca-Cola salesmen, Lou Prentice, as a model, he created a more robust, jolly Santa. It is this image of a twinkling, smiling man that has since defined the American image of Santa.

The Ruston Company created a vinyl-faced Santa holding a small bottle of Coca Cola in his hand in 1958.

Close-ups of uniforms; notice the Lee label.

Buddy Lee was considered one of the most popular dolls in America once. In 1922, it was the second largest doll account in the country. ($250 plus each)

General Mills usually offered toys, not dolls.

One of the most popular premiums were metal decoders like this 1930s-1940s general premium offer. ($35)

The Trix Rabbit was introduced in 1977. ($25)

General Mills offered Sippin' Pals like Sippin' Sue and Sippin' Sam In 1972. They were both dressed in Western garb. ($35 each)

The Honey Nut Cheerios Bee. ($15)

This Quaker Crackels doll, circa 1924, has lasted longer than the Crackels cereal. ($250)

The two versions of Cap'n Crunch. ($25) The one on the right was introduced in 1978, the other in 1989.

The sea captain's costume was based on that of the Louisiana pirate Jean Lafitte.

The later Cap'n Crunch.

Sunshine Animal Crackers used this circus elephant to advertise. It is assumed that this doll dates from the 1930s. There were two versions. ($75)

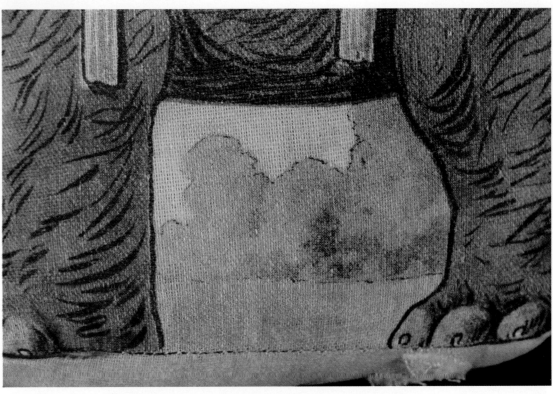

This version had an outdoor scene painted between its legs. Its ears are stamped on and it bears the slogan, "Today! Sunshine Animal crackers at your Grocer." The other version is larger, more three-dimensional and has attached ears and a tail.

The Mack bulldog has been representing Mack trucks since World War I when the British troops called these hardy American vehicles, "bull dogs." ($35)

Whoever dumped the yellow-slickered fisherman pictured in the Star-Kist Tuna can for a smart aleck, fast-talking blue tuna named Charlie was a genius. ($45)

Charlie in cloth and plush. ($35)

The Charlie telephone was offered in 1987 for $19.95 and one Star-Kist label. ($55)

1988 Charlie bank ($25)

1970s Charlie lamp ($45)

Even Charlie is sorry to get on the scale, 1972. ($55)

Smokey the Bear was used by Aim Toothpaste in 1976 to promote their product with this giveaway. ($35)

Smokey came out in many forms. The Aim bear's tag designates him "The official Smokey Bear, licensed U.S. Forest Service. Manufactured by Knickerbocker Toy Company."

His only goal was to prevent forest fires like the one that burned his own paws.

This is Smokey in the 1970s. ($65)

This Ideal, plus-stuffed Smokey became a spokesman for the U.S. Forest Service in 1947. ($65)

Woodsy the Owl was issued by the U.S. Department of Agriculture and became a spokesman against litter in the 1960s. He wanted America to "Give a hoot and don't pollute." ($75)

Nauga was introduced by the Naugahyde Vinyl Fabric Company in 1967. With its oddly shaped face and prominent white eyes, it recalls an owl. Many shops made Nauga dolls from scraps of upholstery so that the surviving dolls come in many sizes. The doll was often a do-it-yourself project. ($65-70)

The Coca Cola Santa changed Americans' image of Santa. This Santa, 1957-'58, is missing his bottle of soda and his pipe. ($125)

Smokey's 50th anniversary celebration began in 1993 and continued through 1994. This is the 50th anniversary Smokey. A portion of the sales were to be donated to the U.S. Forest Service to their Fire Prevention Education Service. ($20)

Consumers were introduced to the Dutch Boy line of paints in 1899. This is a modern version of the Dutch Boy trademark. ($15)

Salty, a brown cloth sailor doll in the shape of a pretzel, was introduced by Nabisco in 1983 ($20)

Action figures: Superman, 1979, D.C. Comics; Remco Toys Spiderman, 1977, Marvel Comics. ($35)

Chapter 5

How Dolls Were Made

The first advertising dolls arrived uncut on a lithographed sheet of material. And since women were used to sewing dolls and making rag dolls, it was a practical and economical idea to let mothers sew and finish the dolls. Not only could they participate in making their children a gift, but the result was a doll that was attractive and affordable. It is important to remember that most of these early advertising dolls cost only a few cents. In the late 1890s and early 1900s, wages averaged between $233 and $486 a year and store-bought fashion dolls sold for $5 to $25. Martha Chase dolls would cost about $10-$18. So an advertising dolls that cost 2-25 cents to cover handling was a real bargain.

It wasn't considered a difficult task for mothers to have to sew these dolls together. Mothers had been making and sewing homemade dolls for their children throughout the nineteenth and twentieth centuries. In addition, throughout the early twentieth century mothers taught their young girls sewing skills by showing them how to sew doll clothes.

In fact, many professional doll makers such as Martha Jenks Chase had gotten their early doll making experience from making rag dolls for their own young children. A Reading, Pennsylvania, doll maker, Mary Hoyer, even issued knitting books giving instructions for knitted doll outfits.

The early dolls arrived with simple instructions printed on the sheet. It was easy to match the pieces, sew the seams, and stuff the finished doll. The recommended stuffing was sawdust, dried beans, or cotton rags. Most of the dolls came in two pieces, a front and back. Some had extra pieces to make shoes, hats and aprons, and tails for animals.

In the 1960s, the Chase Bag Company (no relation to Martha Chase) would forever change the industry with its pre-stuffed cloth dolls, many of which resembled pillows more than dolls. The Chase doll was a one-piece doll with cutout legs and arms.

INSTRUCTIONS FOR

MAKING BODY

Cut out on dash lines (........). Take in the two darts at thigh and the two darts at neck. Lay the printed sides together and sew up all around the body *except* lower end of two legs and a space about six inches long at one side of the body Sew on feet, placing letter "A" of foot pattern to letter "A" of leg pattern, and the same with letter "B."

Turn doll right side out through the opening left on side. Put in card board soles. Begin stuffing at extremities, packing in evenly and tight. Cotton batting makes the best stuffing. Sew up gap and Baby is ready to dress.

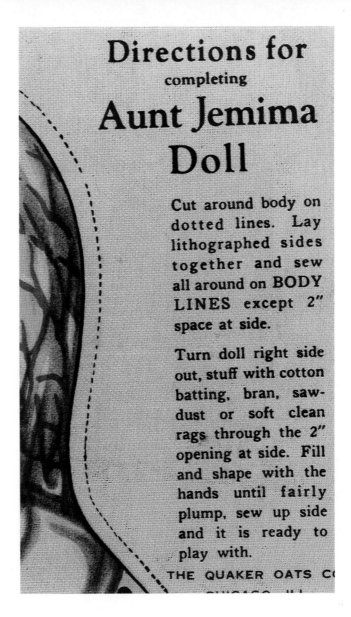

Directions for
completing
Aunt Jemima Doll

Cut around body on dotted lines. Lay lithographed sides together and sew all around on BODY LINES except 2" space at side.

Turn doll right side out, stuff with cotton batting, bran, sawdust or soft clean rags through the 2" opening at side. Fill and shape with the hands until fairly plump, sew up side and it is ready to play with.

THE QUAKER OATS C

The Miss Flaked Rice kit suggests cotton batting as the best stuffing and calls the doll "Baby."

The Aunt Jemima doll is to be stuffed with bran, sawdust, or soft clean rags.

Notice the darts.

Opposite page: Miss Flaked Rice is one of the oldest advertising dolls. She represented an early cereal, Flaked Rice, a product of the American Rice Company. She has more complicated sewing directions than other dolls.

INSTRUCTIONS FOR COMPLETING

OXOL DOLL

Cut out on dotted lines. Place back and front together with colored side out, sew all around except 3" at the top, leaving seam on outside. Stuff comfortably full with cotton batting or sawdust, sew up the opening, trim off surplus seams...shape the doll with the hands, and the OXOL doll is ready for the children's enjoyment...

The Oxol doll.

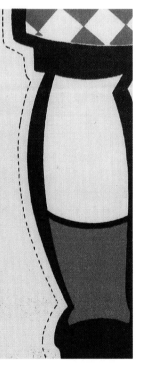

To make your wash white and free from stains add OXOL to the soap and water in tub or machine. Clothes come out whiter than soap alone could ever make them. Stains disappear, germs are killed too. OXOL also works like magic removing stains on tile and porcelain. Use it in your cleaning water and work will be much easier. Try OXOL today. Your grocer has it, a big bottle for a small price.

© 1931 J. L. PRESCOTT CO.
PASSAIC, N. J.

Notice the ad for Oxol on the doll.

Instructions for Crinkle the Cat.

Kellogg's
Colorful
Cloth
Dolls

YOU WILL
WANT ALL FOUR

FRECKLES The Frog
DANDY The Duck
DINKEY The Dog
CRINKLE The Cat

If your grocer cannot supply
you with the doll you want,
mail one package top from
KELLOGG'S WHEAT
KRISPIES and 10c to Dept.
C. D., Kellogg Company,
Battle Creek, Michigan. For
the four dolls, send four
package tops and 25c in
coin.

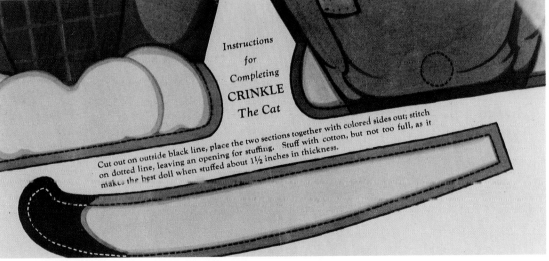

Instructions
for
Completing
CRINKLE
The Cat

Cut out on outside black line, place the two sections together with colored sides out; stitch on dotted line, leaving an opening for stuffing. Stuff with cotton, but not too full, as it makes the best doll when stuffed about 1½ inches in thickness.

This doll comes with an attachable tail.

These dolls used to come in mailing envelopes such as this.

INSTRUCTIONS

Cut along outer edge of printing, place the two sections together with colored sides out; stitch on dotted line, leaving an opening for stuffing. Stuff with cotton to about 1 inch in thickness. Fine made up as "bean-bags" too! Can be stuffed with Beans, Dried Peas, or Sawdust.

The dolls could simply be glorified bean bags.

Mailings came with additional offers.

This Gretchen, a doll offered by Little Crow Foods to promote Coco Wheat Ceareals, is sewn with an outside outline stitch rather than being sewn inside out. Those who finished these dolls had varied sewing expertise. Gretchen was advertised on cereal boxes from 1949-1966.

Back of doll.

Notice the differences in coloration in the doll from its pristine mint, uncut version to the used and well-used versions. Colors faded drastically.

Chapter 6

Young Girls' Playthings Come of Age

It was the Ideal Novelty and Toy Company that probably redefined the doll's image in the 1940s. Most dolls had been babies or young, toddler-like playmates until then. It was Ideal that conceived the idea of the new fashion doll, a doll which catered to a young girl's idea of becoming an adult. Being a grown-up meant having breasts and wearing makeup and glamorous party clothes. It was Ideal's Revlon dolls that set the stage for the Barbie doll.

After the initial success of the Teddy Bear in 1902 rocketed the Ideal Novelty and Toy Company (see Chapter 9) to success, the Ideal company then looked for another blockbuster doll. The company hit the jackpot again in 1933 with another million-dollar idea, a Shirley Temple doll, a doll based on the famous child actress. By 1938, sales of the Shirley Temple dolls totaled more than six million dollars.

Ideal's next best seller was the 1949 Toni doll, a doll that could be given her own home permanent. The doll was designed by Bernard Lipfert, who was also responsible for the designs of EFF and BEES's Patsy, Madame Alexander's Dionne Quintuplets, and the Shirley Temple doll. Toni was introduced on September 5, 1950. She came with her own home permanent kit, hair curlers, wrapping papers, and comb. Toni came in several sizes ranging from 14 to 20 inches. To help the hair of these dolls survive their frequent shampoos, the Ideal company enlisted the help of chemists at DuPont to create a new hair fiber. The new Toni doll cost $9.95. Today, in mint condition, she sells for several hundred dollars.

Toni dolls were the rage of young girls in the 1940s and 1950s and Ideal's management decided to capitalize on her popularity. Toni Twins appeared everywhere asking the question, "Which twin has the Toni?

Beginning in 1951. Ideal introduced four other dolls using the same Toni body — Miss Curity, Mary Hartline, Betsy McCall, and Harriet Hubbard Ayer. Besides the Aunt Jemima doll, which was patented in 1914, 1916, and 1917, the Toni Doll and Miss Curity were the only other advertising dolls to be patented. The Toni doll was patented in 1949 and Miss Curity in 1951.

Mary Hartline was based on television's golden-haired cowgirl, Mary Hartline. She was a popular band leader who dressed in a red majorette outfit with white boots.

Miss Curity came out in 1949. The first lady of First Aid was dressed in a white nurse's outfit and came with a nurse's kit and instructions on using Curity bandages. She was first manufactured in 1949 and was made of hard plastic with a swivel neck and jointed legs and arms. In 1953, Sears offered another Miss Curity doll. This doll and her accessories sold for $11.95 when new. In 1953, another company manufactured a tiny, 7-inch doll with a one-piece body and legs. A 20-inch doll was issued later in the 1950s and a 19-1/2 inch molded display doll was offered later.

Ideal introduced the Betsy McCall doll in 1952 to advertise McCall patterns. Betsy originated as a paper doll and was first shown in the May 1951 issue of McCall's magazine. The first Betsy McCall doll was vinyl, with brown hair and round sleep eyes.

The Ayer doll was manufactured in 1953 to promote Harriet Hubbard Ayer's line of cosmetics. The doll came with her own set of cosmetics. Ayer began her career as an interior decorator in New York City in the 1880s. In order to earn more money to support her two daughters, she entered the cosmetics business. Her first successful item was cold cream. In 1893 she was declared insane by her daughters in a fight over money. She managed to get herself released a short time later, and sold her rights to the business. The new management contracted with Ideal to produce a Harriet Hubbard Ayer doll, but soon afterward the cosmetic line disappeared from the market. The doll came in four sizes — 14, 15, 18-1/2 and 20-1/2 inches. She has a hard vinyl body with movable limbs. Her long fingernails are painted red.

Another hard plastic doll was Miss Sunbeam, a sweet-faced young blonde with curls piled high on her head who has been the symbol of Sunbeam Bread since 1942, when she was created by E. Segner, a well-known Greenwich Village artist. She was introduced as a trademark doll in 1959 by the Minnesota-based bakery. Her face was copied from the image found on bread package wrappers. The Sunbeam doll was manufactured by Eegee. A second doll was introduced in the 1970s and recently a third cloth doll was introduced to promote the product. This doll comes with a note asking its owner to love it and hug it. It is interesting to compare the manufacture of the three dolls and note the decline in quality and details.

In 1950, the Miss Revlon dolls forever changed the image of dolls and marked the end of innocence for America's little girls. The Miss Revlon dolls were also products of the Ideal Novelty and Toy Company. In 1950 the Revlon Company made a deal with Ideal to produce a series of fashion dolls to promote Revlon cosmetics The Revlon dolls became some of the most beautifully dressed dolls of the time. Revlon dolls were produced until 1958 and by then four different styles had been produced. The earliest doll was a 10-1/2 inch Little Miss Revlon. She had pierced ears, high-heeled shoes and a swivel waist. In 1956, a larger doll was introduced. In 1958, there were two more

Miss Revlons, an 18-inch doll and a 19-inch Mrs. Revlon doll. The Mrs. Revlon came with a gray wig and purple eye shadow.

The Revlon dolls came with many different outfits ranging from fancy ball dresses to party frocks to ordinary house dresses. The dresses reflect the feminine thrust of 1950s fashions — pinched-in waists, tight bodices, full crinolines, and high heels.

Mary Hoyer, a Reading, Pennsylvania,. doll maker, made this lovely composition doll in the 1930s and 1940s. ($350 plus)

Another Mary Hoyer doll with a knitted skater's outfit. ($400 plus)

Another version of the Mary Hoyer knitted dress. ($450 plus)

The Toni doll by Ideal started an advertising/marketing revolution in 1949. New she sold for $9.95. Today, in mint condition, she sells for $200 plus.

She came with her own home permanent kit.

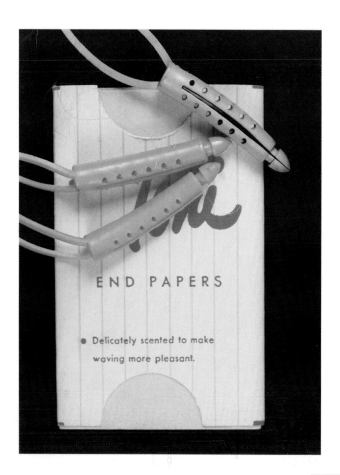

Curlers and end papers.

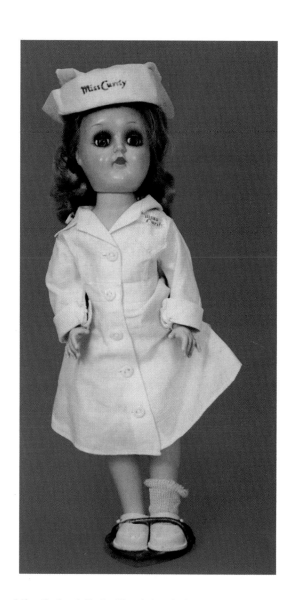

Miss Curity doll, the First lady of First Aid 1951. ($200)

Harriet Hubbard Ayer doll in 1953 advertising cosmetics. ($200)

The 1950 Little Miss Revlon. ($220)

Carol the Color Me doll invited young girls to try to play with makeup. Fashion Two Twenty Cosmetics issued this sales incentive in 1969. Five color-on wipe-off crayons came along with the doll to color the hair, the eyes, and the clothing. ($75)

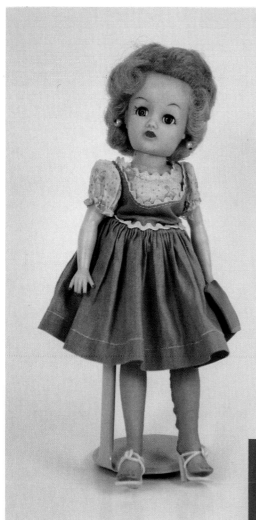

The Revlon dolls were always well dressed.
($200-250)

For a summer party.

For a party.

Another housedress for everyday wear. Notice the hair and shoes.

A day dress. Many dolls came with a Miss Revlon label.

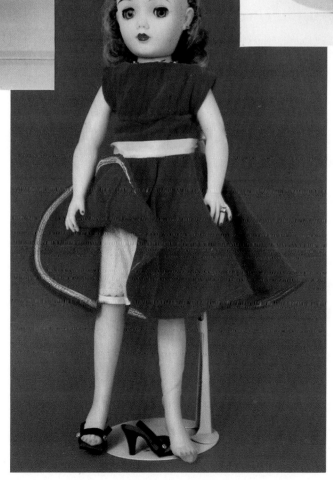

The Queen of Diamonds, complete with a diamond ring, earrings, and necklace.

The Queen of Pearls. ($225)

The first Betsy McCall doll by Ideal. It is marked McCall corp on the back of its head. ($125)

One of the earliest Betsy McCall dolls. ($320)

Another Betsy McCall doll. This doll is unmarked and made of hard plastic. Since the age of Miss Revlons, there have been many other young girl advertising dolls. While some have been made out of composition and hard plastic, most have been manufactured out of cloth. Companies today have found, just as their early twentieth century counterparts did, that cloth dolls are not only economical to produce and market, but they make very good "cuddly friends." And they are a very durable plaything. ($150)

Miss Sunbeam, 1959.($55)

A cloth Miss Sunbeam from the 1980s. ($15)

In 1990, another Swiss Miss was offered in a smaller size. Notice the differences in details. The later doll has a vinyl face. ($20)

A 1978 Swiss Miss. The powdered chocolate drink mix company has used a blonde girl with pigtails since 1960. In 1972, she became a puppet. In 1977, the first cloth doll premium was offered. This doll came with a child-sized playhouse, patterned after a Swiss chalet. The playhouse was made out of heavy duty corrugated cardboard. ($25)

A Kool Aid kid on the package.

Kool-Aid kids have represented the drink mix since 1953. This is a Kool-Aid kid from the 1980s. ($25)

Little Debbie 1987. ($55 with box)

The 30th anniversary doll offer.

Miss North American World Wide Movers, another Barbie look-alike from the 1980s. ($35)

Miss Jordache — a Barbie look-alike goes into advertising in the 1980s. ($25)

Primsy Rose is a Jammie Pie from the magical "Land of Sweet Dreams," manufactured by Playskool in 1986. ($15)

Blue Bonnet Sue, 1980s. ($25)

The Lysol Kids, a yellow-haired baby and a brown haired older brother, made in 1986 by Trudy Corp. ($25 each)

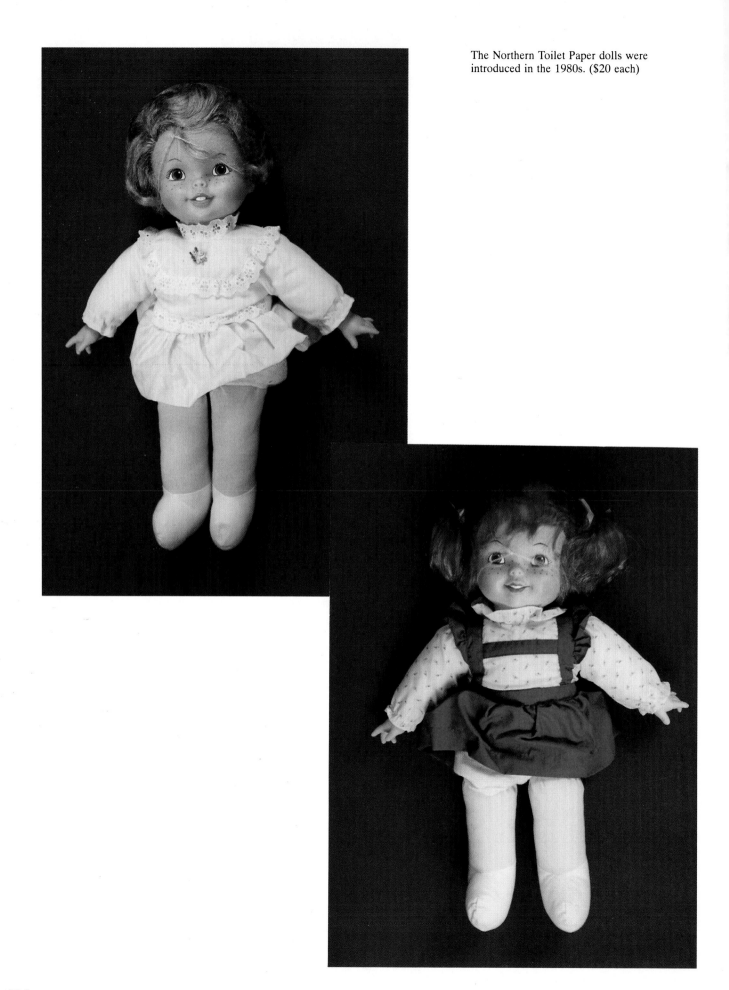

The Northern Toilet Paper dolls were introduced in the 1980s. ($20 each)

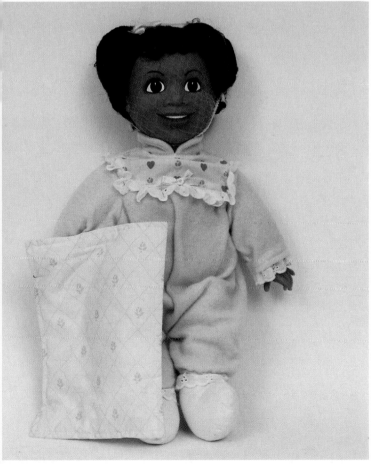

Hallmark Cards introduced a series of famous American women dolls in the 1970s. ($35)

A new wave of cloth dolls were introduced in the 1970s by the Chase Bag Company and a new age of trademark promotions was launched.

Chapter 7

Madison Avenue Enters
the Game and
Simplifies Doll Images

Cloth advertising dolls were never pre-stuffed prior to 1960, but that would change in 1963 when the Chase Bag Company in Reidsville, N.C., (no relation to the company founded in the mid-1800s by Martha Jenks Chase) entered the doll business. Their first order came from the Leo Burnett Advertising Agency in Chicago. Burnett wanted 75,000 dolls. The doll was the Jolly Green Giant. It was to be printed on green cloth with black detailing and a red mouth. Printing red ink over green was a problem since the colors ran and the resulting color kept on turning out brown. Eventually the company solved the problem and the Green Giant was born. Before that ad promotion had ended, Chase Bag had produced more than 600,000 Green Giant dolls.

Kelloggs contacted Chase next and asked the company to manufacture a Woody Woodpecker and a Toucan Sam. Little Sprout followed, providing a friend for the Jolly Green Giant and a new collectible for doll lovers. By the end of the year, the Chase Bag Company had made a half a million Woody Woodpeckers, 400,000 Toucan Sams, and millions of Green Giants and Little Sprouts.

Chase's big moment came in the late 1960s when the company entered into a contract with McDonald's and began to produce Ronald McDonald. Ronald McDonald would eventually become the most popular promotional doll ever produced. By the time the company received a contract for Hamburglar, the Chase Bag Company had sent more than one million dolls a year to the customers of what was then the largest fast food company in the United States.

Then, in 1967, the company began to produce a thousand Mr. Peanuts weekly in three different sizes.

Burger King introduced three versions of the Burger King doll. The first was introduced in 1972 and is a 16-inch fat pillow caricature of a King. In 1973, a similar-looking doll was introduced. The only difference between the two is that the early one has an unmarked medallion on his chest, the latter has "Burger King" printed on the medallion.

With orders for 700,000 of the short, fat Burger Kings, 300,000 Pillsbury Doughboys, 150,000 Hardee's Gilbert Giddy Up and more Ronald McDonalds and Dairy Queen Kids, the Chase Bag Company was the largest producer of cloth dolls. The Chase Bag Company continued as the biggest manufacturer in the country through the 1980s. During its heyday, it was not uncommon for Chase to receive

and process orders for hundreds of thousands of dolls each week.

Chase entered the doll business in 1963, one hundred years after it was founded in Boston to recycle gunny sacks. Chase recycled sacks used to import cocoa beans, coffee, and raw sugar to the United States. With the invention of the sewing machine, the founding brothers Henry, Thomas, and H. Lincoln Chase began to manufacture their own bags at a lower cost. In 1866 Francis Luddington joined the firm and developed new markets in St. Louis and Kansas City, eventually branching out into the Midwest and South.

The company went out of business in the 1980s.

Among Chase's other contributions to the advertising world were Alice from MD Bathroom Tissue; Allergic Annie from Honeywell; Bazooka Joe of bubble gum fame; Big Boy the hamburger eater and his friends Dolly, Nugget, and Scarecrow Sam for Brach's Candy; Charlie Chocks for Chocks Vitamins; Chiquita Banana; C. and H. Sugar Twins; Eskimo Boy for Eskimo Pie; Fun Fair clowns for Kellogg's; Hot Tamale Kid for Hot Tamale Candies; Jack Frost in three versions for Jack Frost sugar; Lerner Newsboy for Myers Publishing; Little Hans for Nestles Chocolate; Mohawk Tommy for Mohawk carpet; Mr. Magoo for General Electric; Patient Pat for Kimberley Clark; Punchy for Hawaiian Punch; Raisin for Ralston Purina's Raising Bran, and Tasty for Tastykake.

What makes Chase Dolls distinctive is the simplicity of their design. Chase had artists who changed designs sent from advertising agencies so that the dolls could be cut and sewn in one piece. One of the distinguishing characteristics of a Chase doll was the simplicity of its graphics. Chase dolls were similar in outline to the designs used in coloring books. Most Chase dolls were designed in one piece, usually a simple triangular shape, and generally the arms and legs were cut free from the body. Their facial features were simple line curves or circles.

By the time the company stopped making dolls it had transformed some of America's most familiar and popular trademark images into dolls.

Mattel also entered the cloth advertising doll world with its happy trio of Shoppin' Pals — Cracker Jack boy, the Chicken of the Sea Mermaid, and the Morton Salt Girl.

Three Cracker Jack dolls are known to exist, one produced in 1917, one in 1974, and another in the 1980s. The

The first was 16 inches and cost 50 cents and three labels or $2.50 and no labels. It was manufactured in 1966 and was the first doll produced by Chase Bag. ($30) The second Green Giant was 28 inches tall and was made in 1973. ($25) A 6-1/2 inch vinyl Sprout was manufactured in 1971.($10) A 10-inch cloth Sprout came out in 1973. ($25) There was a 24-inch inflatable Sprout in 1976.

Part of the Chase Bag Company legacy.

Two cloth variations on Little Sprout ($25)

The whole family of Green Giants and Sprouts.

Little Sprout in cloth, plush and vinyl. ($10)

1917 doll was manufactured by Ideal and wears a white sailor suit and carries box of Cracker Jack. The 1974 version is 15 inches high and was manufactured by Mattel. Named Sailor Jack, he has lithographed features and orange hair and wears a blue sailor suit and white sailor hat. He carries a tiny box of Cracker Jack. The most recent is a 1980 vinyl doll made by Vogue Dolls. Cracker Jack is now a trademark of Borden, Inc.

Morton offered its first doll in the early 1970s. She was an 8-inch vinyl doll wearing plastic boots and a rain slicker. In 1974 Mattel made a 14-inch Morton Salt doll. It sold for $4 and has mitten-shaped hands and yarn hair, wears a yellow dress, and comes with a small box of Morton salt.

Chicken of the Sea tuna is a product of the Ralston Purina Company. Since the 1960s, there have been two mermaid dolls that have represented the product. The first was issued in the mid 1960s and is vinyl from the waist up. The lower part is cloth. The second version is pre-stuffed cloth, one of Mattel Shoppin' Pals made in 1974.

Three versions of Ronald McDonald, a character which eventually
became the most popular promotional doll ever produced. ($15)

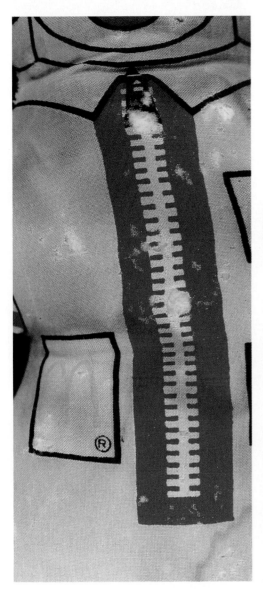

The first McDonald doll had a black zipper tag, 1971-1972.

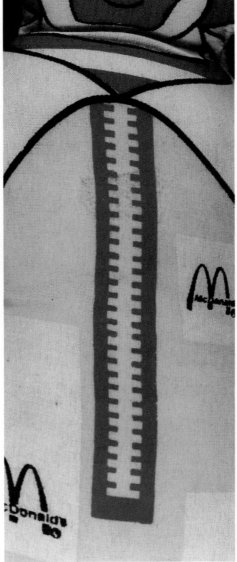

There was no zipper tag on the 1977 version.

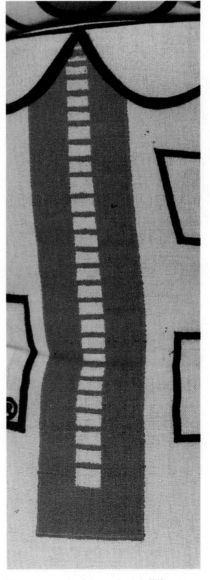

There were no zipper tag and different pockets on the 1972-1973 version.

Hamburglar. ($25 with cloak, $20 without)

The short, fat Burger Kings. One has a plain medallion. The other has company name. ($10)

The Burger King.

The company introduced another version of the doll in 1977. This one is taller, thinner, has a red mustache and beard, and is a more realistic king. ($20)

Hardee's Gilbert Giddyup was offered in 1971. ($20)

The Texas Dairy Queen offered this Dairy Queen Kid in 1974. He had three friends, Sweet Nell, Cheerleader, and Funfighter McDoom. ($20)

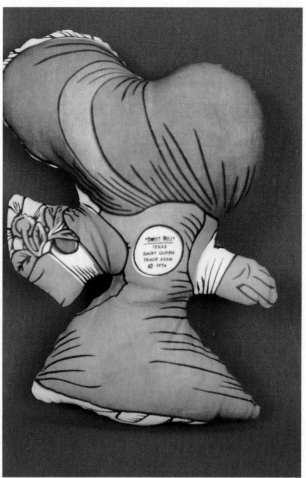

Sweet Nell.

Mr. Peanut. ($20)

The Doughboy, front and back.

The Independent Grocer's Association offered the IGA Tablerite Kid, a 12-inch doll, in the late 1970s or early 1980s. ($20)

A cowboy, Tablerite Kid holds a gun ready to draw and wears a large brimmed white hat.

Junior Mints, a product of Nabisco, introduced The Fonz, a look-a-like doll for a character in the television sitcom "Happy Days." The offer ran from November 1976 through May 1977 and was first advertised in T.V. Guide Magazine. The doll is unique in that it bears the lithographed face of a real man, actor Henry Winkler. ($25)

Mattel issued a Captain Kangaroo doll in the 1970s based on the star of a children's television show. ($25)

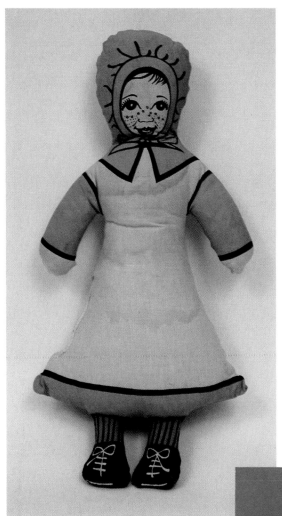

Herald Press's doll came out in 1971. She is 16 inches tall and her apron is marked on the back with "Herald Press 1971." ($25)

The Allied doll was created in the 1970s by Allied Van Lines. She is 17 inches, made of stamped cloth, and wears an orange jumper with the Allied Van insignia. ($25)

Allergic Annie was a promotional doll from Honeywell Company, the Cleaner Air people. She carries a flower and has tears dripping down her face. One arm is cut free, the other is stamped on her jumper. She has red weepy eyes and a red puffy nose. It is unusual to have such a sad doll as a promotional item. ($35)

Marjorie Merritt Darrah decided to advertise the Mary Merritt Doll Museum, her doll museum in Douglasville, Pennsylvania, with a promotional doll in 1974. It is dressed in a style similar to Amish women, but obviously in a more colorful red. ($15)

These dolls used similar designs and outfits.

An unmarked doll in a similar costume. ($15)

Another unmarked doll ($15)

Amish dolls are a popular design. Authentic Amish dolls are dressed in dark colors, maroons, blacks, grays, or navy blues, the colors favored by the "Plain Folk." In keeping with the biblical injunction of Deuteronomy, some Amish don't put faces on their dolls because they fear it offends God by making a "graven" image.($35 each)

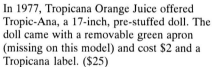

In 1977, Tropicana Orange Juice offered Tropic-Ana, a 17-inch, pre-stuffed doll. The doll came with a removable green apron (missing on this model) and cost $2 and a Tropicana label. ($25)

Tasty, the Tastykake baker, was introduced on the package in 1974. It cost $1 with a coupon. Tastykakes are manufactured by the Tasty Baking Company in Philadelphia. ($15)

This is the third Chiquita doll and was offered as a mail-in premium in 1974. It was mass-produced and offered in women's magazines and the Sunday comics. When new it cost $1.75 plus two seals from Chiquita bananas. ($35)

The idea for Big Boy, a chubby little boy, was intended to capitalize on the chain's claim of having the largest hamburgers. The restaurant chain was founded in 1936 by Bob Wain in Glendale, California. The name came about when customers would walk in and ask for the "big one." Eventually the owner decided to franchise his hamburger restaurant under the name Big Boy. In 1967, the franchise was sold to Willard J. Marriot. Big Boy Restaurants recently announced plans to slim down and modernize its trademark, the Big Boy. ($20)

In 1978, two new dolls were introduced Dolly —a small girl holding a big boy behind her back, and a dog, Nugget.($20 each) The dolls were 14 inches high and cost $3.98 each when new. Through the years there have been many variations on the doll. Big Boy has appeared in vinyl ($35) and as various gimmick toys such as a night light ($75) and in two forms of cloth doll. The earliest Big Boy doll is 17 inches tall. The later version is more like a pillow and is 14 inches high.

Notice the similarity between the back views of Dolly and Diana, Aunt Jemima's daughter.

Christian K. Nelson had a brainstorm in 1921 to market a combination of ice-cream and chocolate in a bar. In the 1930s, the Eskimo Pie Corporation began to use a figure in Eskimo clothing. The first Eskimo Boy cloth doll was manufactured in 1964. ($25)

Kellogg introduced a series of three unmarked Fun Fair clowns in 1973. ($25)

Eskimo Boy was modified in 1975 and marked Eskimo Pie. ($25)

Hot Tamale Candies offered the Tamale Kid from 1967 to 1975. The older, 18-inch dolls were $1.25. The later 16-inch dolls cost $1.35. ($25)

Hot Tamale Kid

A smiling, blue-suited Jack Frost was first introduced in either the late 1960s or early 1970s to represent Jack Frost Sugar. The first doll was 18 inches tall and wears a blue snow suit with a diamond. The name Jack Frost is on his blue and white stocking cap. ($25)

The next doll was 20 inches tall with his name on his pocket. Notice the differences in clothing and hair styles. ($25)

Little Hans (Nestles) was made by Chase in 1970 to show the chocolate company's Swiss background. ($25)

Myers Publishing issued the Lerner Newsboy in 1970. It issued a Lerner Newspup in 1972. ($25)

The latest Jack Frost was a Christmas promotion in 1975 and cost $1.50 new. He is not marked with the company name and is the rarest of the three. ($35)

A Native American Mohawk Tommy was chosen as a trademark by Mohawk carpet. ($25)

Punchy became the Hawaiian Punch mascot in 1961 when he was created by a Los Angeles ad agency. He appeared on the radio and asked, "How would you like a Hawaiian punch?" Punchy made his television debut on the Jack Paar Show in 1963. He appeared with his sidekick, Oaf, and the two did a skit which ended with Punchy giving Oaf a resounding blow. Punchy was replaced by a Hawaiian Hula girl in 1966, but reinstated soon thereafter. He was semi-retired in the 1980s and then revived in 1988. Company officials called him the best spokesman ever. The 1961 promotion doll, like the Big Boy dolls, is more pillow than doll. ($35)

Mr. Magoo for General Electric. ($25)

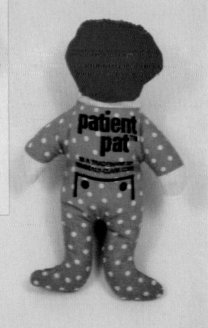

Patient Pat for Kimberley Clark. ($20)

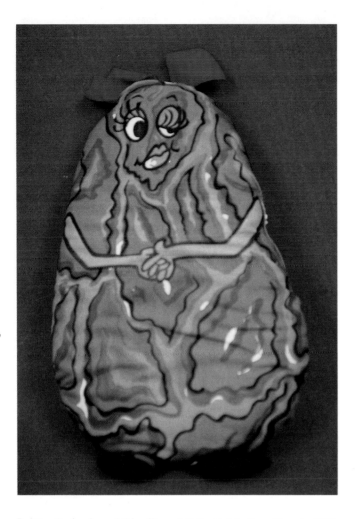

Ralston Purina issued this pillow doll for Raisin Bran Chex in 1973. ($25)

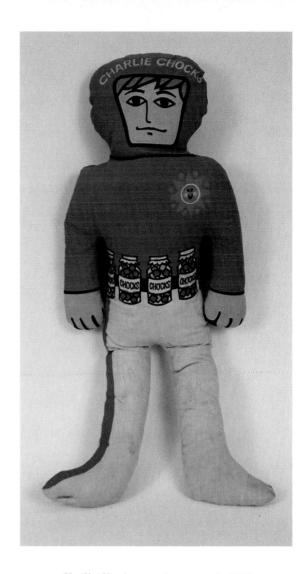

Charlie Chocks was given away in 1970 and 1971 to promote Chocks, a multivitamin for children. The 20-inch doll is dressed in a pink space suit with a belt of Chocks bottles around his waist. He cost $1 new. ($25)

Ralston Purina issued the Scarecrow doll in 1965, made of cloth with a vinyl face. ($30)

The California and Hawaiian Sugar Company produced a set of boy and girl Hawaiian Twins in 1971. Each doll was sold for $1 plus an oval from the package. The first ad appeared in 1971. It was extended twice to 1972 and 1973. ($25 each)

Pepperidge Farms issued a Gingerman and a Goldfish in the 1970s to promote cookies and crackers with the same names. ($25 each)

Ludens' 5th Avenue candies issued another pillow in the 1970s
($30)

Baron von Esskay was offered by the
Esskay Meat Company of Baltimore. He is
dressed like a World War I flying ace. ($25)
($25)

Pops-rite popcorn. ($25)

Brown's chicken was a Midwestern and Southern fast food chain. The first Farmer Brown was 18 inches high and was offered in the mid-1970s. In 1978, the chain offered a smaller, 16-inch farmer and an 11-inch companion, Brewster Rooster. The dolls were available at the restaurants and sold new for $1. (Large farmer, $55; small, $45; rooster, $25)

The Revere Ware man is dressed like Paul Revere in a Colonial uniform. ($25)

1970s The McDonald Girl ($25)

This raccoon was a souvenir of the 1980 Lake Placid Winter Olympics. ($25)

Freddie the Fireman ($15)

This dour faced Coors man represents the Colorado beer company. ($25)

FREDDIE FIREMAN®

The U.S. Mailman is one of many Postal Service promotion dolls. ($15)

A Philadelphia Flyer's hockey player ($15)

A Dodgers doll. ($15)

Benjamin Franklin represents the Franklin Life Insurance Company for a 1970s promotion. ($25)

These trademark children can still be seen on Eat It All ice cream cone dispensers. ($25 each)

The Dorney Park clown was called Alfundo by its founders, the Ott Family. The doll was used for many years as a symbol of the Allentown Amusement Park in Pennsylvania. ($125)

The Morton Salt girl and the slogan, "When it rains, it pours" date from 1914. The 14-inch Mattel doll was offered in 1974 and sold for $4 in 1974. The doll carries a small Morton salt box.

Mattel also entered the cloth advertising doll world in 1974 with its happy trio of shoppin' pals — the Cracker Jack boy, the Chicken of the Sea Mermaid, and the Morton Salt Girl. ($25 each)

Today Cracker Jack is a product of the Borden Company. Three dolls are known to exist, one produced in 1917, one in 1974, and the third in the 1980s. The first doll was manufactured by Ideal, wears a white sailor suit, and carries a box of Cracker Jack. The 1974 version is 15 inches high and was manufactured by Mattel. Named Sailor Jack, he has lithographed features, wears a navy blue uniform, and carries a tiny box of Cracker Jack.

The Chicken of the Sea Mermaid is a product of the Ralston Purina Company. Here are two of the dolls that have represented the product. One, a pre-stuffed cloth doll, was one of the Mattel Shoppin' Pals. The second one is from the 1980s. ($25)

The Knickerbocher Company, which manufactured Smokey Bear, Raggedy Anns and Andys, and many other character dolls, produced the Levi Strauss rag dolls in 1974. The dolls came in three sizes. ($10-25 depending on size)

Western Union introduced Dolly Grams on February 16, 1975. These small, handmade, velvet-covered dolls with raffia hair carried one of nineteen messages saying "Happy Birthday," "Happy Day," "Please Cheer Up," or "Just Want to Say" on their pockets. The dolls were advertised as alternatives to a telegram. ($15 each)

A message bearing animal from the 1980s.

Brach's Candy introduced two clowns. This one named Luv ($25) dates from 1968 and came with a small cloth children's book. ($25; $30 with book)

A page from the book.

Chapter 8

Fast Food Mania
Creates New Doll Market

Carhop restaurants sprang up throughout California in 1940s and 1950s about the same time as Americans began their love affair with the automobile. California's climate also contributed to the popularity of convertible tops.

So when Dick and Mac McDonald opened their California barbecue restaurant in 1940 and hired carhop waitresses they helped kick off a lifestyle revolution that would forever change America's eating habits, beginning a trend that would eventually take Americans out of their kitchens and into their cars for a fast-food stop. "Eating on the run" would become an American way of life.

Initially the McDonalds hired carhops and eliminated menus, silverware, and plates to cut costs. In 1948, they streamlined even more by creating the first self-service hamburger stand with a three-item menu — hamburgers, french fries, and soft drinks. In 1954, the McDonalds attracted the attention of Ray Kroc, a milkshake-mixer distributor who would create the multi-million dollar idea of a fast food franchise. It was Kroc who saw tremendous marketing potential in the McDonald's restaurant and made a deal to handle the franchises of the McDonald idea. In 1961, he bought out the brothers for a song, then created one of the most successful food service phenomenons of the twentieth century.

Ronald McDonald made his first appearance as a company mascot in 1963. In 1966, the company introduced its spokesman clown at store events. Five years later, the Chase Bag Company created the Ronald McDonald doll. This orange and yellow cloth doll became the most popular selling doll in America. The McDonald doll was slightly modified and offered again in 1974. It cost $1.25. A smaller doll, the third, was introduced in 1977. Hamburglar, a black-and-white striped doll with a detachable cape, was introduced in 1972. McDonald's went vinyl in 1976, promoting seven McDonaldland characters — Ronald McDonald, Big Mac, Grimace, Mayor McCheese, Captain Crook, and the Professor. In the years since McDonald's has issued toy promotions relating to current Disney movies, popular cartoon characters, and pop icons.

Wendy's was established in 1969 by R. David Thomas. Although Thomas's trademark girl with blond pigtails was based on his own daughter, he never created a trademark doll, choosing instead to use popular carton characters with no link to the product. For instance, there was a 1990 campaign with Alf figures and other small animals like the Furrskins, the Purr-tenders, and wildlife animals.

Other food chains such as Chicken Delight, Burger King, Chuck E. Cheese, and Pizza Hut have followed suit. In the past few years, Christmas has become one of the biggest doll and character promotion seasons for fast food chains.

The founder of the fast food feast. ($20)

Remco produced seven McDonaldland characters in 1976. This is Ronald and the Professor. ($10 each)

Sesame Street goes to McDonald's. Miss Piggy 1980s. ($10)

Kermit the Frog and Baby Kermit.($10 each)

Miss Piggy with Fozzie

Grimace made his first appearance with Ronald McDonald in 1971. This figure dates from the 1980s. ($10)

One of the mice from Disney's movie "Cinderella," 1980's. ($10)

Kermit in ski sweater and scarf

Dinosaurs became popular in the 1980s after a series of record-breaking dinosaur movies. ($5)

More Wendy's Furrskins from Christmas 1987.

Wendy's Furrskins. ($10 each)

Matthew Groening created Bart Simpson and his family in 1990. Bart Simpson wowed America. He was everywhere, on television and immortalized in plastic. He was quickly adopted by the Burger King Corporation and in 1990 Simpson dolls were offered in a special promotion. ($10)

Wendy's went environmental in 1988 and began to promote the World Wildlife Federation with a series of wild animals. ($10)

Alfie helps sell Burger Kings in 1988. ($10)

Another Alfie helps sell burgers.

Burger King Purr-tenders. 1988. ($10)

The Peanuts family is a popular endorser of products for children, associated with everything from Avon to soaps to Burger King. ($25 the set).

Ted E. Bear, a 1987 giveaway ($5)

Chapter 9

Bears Join the Party

Ironically the leading manufacturer of composition dolls, the Ideal Novelty and Toy Company, owes its beginnings to a bear, a Teddy Bear. These humble beginnings can be traced to the year 1902 when Ideal's founding father, Morris Michtom, asked Teddy Roosevelt for permission to use his name on a bear doll. And it was the "Teddy" Bear that began a new trend towards playable, asexual dolls, that could be held, cuddled and played with rather than admired from afar.

Teddy Bears owe their existence to a fluke. President Theodore Roosevelt loved to hunt and went on many African safaris. On a bear hunt in 1902, his Mississippi guides, hoping to win his favor, captured an old bear, tied it to a tree, and offered it to the president. Roosevelt refused to shoot the bear. A cartoonist picked up on the idea and drew "Teddy's Bear."

Michtom realized he had a hot item and immediately made a small, plush bear and mailed the sample to the White House, asking the president if he could use his name. The president replied, "I don't think my name is likely to be worth much in the bear business, but you are welcome to use it," and so the Teddy Bear was born as well as the Ideal Novelty and Toy Company.

Teddy bears have been used as advertising premiums in almost every industry to promote products ranging from orange juice, cereals, and ice cream to oil companies, banks, news magazines, department stores and supermarkets. Among other companies using bears is Bradlee's, which produced plush gold bears with big plastic eyes; Close Up Toothpaste bears, which came out in 1977 and had velcro paws; the Domino Sugar Bear; the 1975 Icee Bear; the 1968 Tide Bear; the 1967 Travelodge Sleepy Bear, and the A&W Great Root Bear.

These Maxwell House Coffee Bears were introduced in 1971 for $4.95. They wear a red striped nightcap and come in three sizes. ($25 each)

The 1972 Snow Crop Teddy advertised Snow Crop orange juice. "Hi, I'm Teddy Snow Crop." The doll is made out of terry cloth with a gray vinyl face. ($65)

A teddy bear.

A Teddy Bear puppet.

The Scrungy Bear promoted Shop-Rite supermarkets in 1971. ($20)

Another Shop-Rite Bear. ($10)

Scrungy Bear in 1988. ($15)

The Lyon's Cubs. ($15 each)

The Kodak Bear, 1989 ($10)

Two bears promoting Meridian Bank (Reading, Pennyslvania), 1988. ($15)

L.L. Bean in Freeport, Maine had their own backbacking bear in the 1980s. ($35)

Channel 39, Bethlehem, Pennyslvania, issued teddy bears in a navy sweater and a maroon sweater in the 1980s. The television station also gave out Sesame Street characters such as Ernie to contributors. ($25)

The Coco Bear Breakfast buddy was a premium for Little Crow Foods' Coco Wheat cereal. ($15)

A Juicy Fruit candy bear from the Heide Candy company, 1988. ($15)

The Snuggle Bear promotes Snuggle fabric softener. ($10)

The Sara Lee Bagel bear ($25)

A Mott Apple juice Apple of My Eye bear, 1988. ($10)

1988 Christmas offering from Bloomingdale's department store. ($25)

The Aramis bear ($10)

The Getty (oil) Teddy ($10)

The Avon Bear ($10)

The Hershey's's Teddy ($30)

Another Hershey's bear makes life bearable. ($15)

M & M's bear ($15)

Time magazine bear ($10)

The Sugar Bear was the only doll known to be used by Post cereal with a product tie-in. It was first introduced in 1972 and was used to advertise Super Sugar Crisp and Super Orange Crisp Cereals. ($10)

A musical 1990 Christmas Sugar Bear. When the bear's stomach is pressed it sings three Christmas songs. ($10)

The Sears Craftsman bear, 1980s, came with safety glasses. ($20)

The Klondike Bears ($25)

Burpee Bearpee ($25)

AT&T telephone bear ($10)

Sugar Bear ($10)

Even the Japanese know the power of a cuddly bear. This bear was part of a promotion for the Japanese train system offered in the late 1980s. ($10)

Be-Ro flour bear from Scotland ($10)

Snickers bear ($10)

Chapter 10

Dolls Go Plush

Companies have experimented with doll-making materials since the early 1900s, but it is universally agreed that cuddly, soft dolls are the most popular among all ages of children. The first plush animals appeared as early as the 1950s. Most of these dolls were animals such as Nestle's Quik Rabbit, the True Temper Eager Beaver, and the Maxwell House bears. In the 1980s, companies began to produce lush, vividly colored animals and cartoon characters such as the Mott Apple of Your Eye pets, the fanciful Dole Bananimals, and the Del Monte Country Yumkins.

Blue Bonnet margarine has used several dolls. This cow was introduced in the 1980s. ($10)

In 1989, Dole introduced the Dole animal pals — Dole Bananapus, the Bananabear, Bananarilla, and Bananasaur. ($10 each)

The Bananimal Banabear

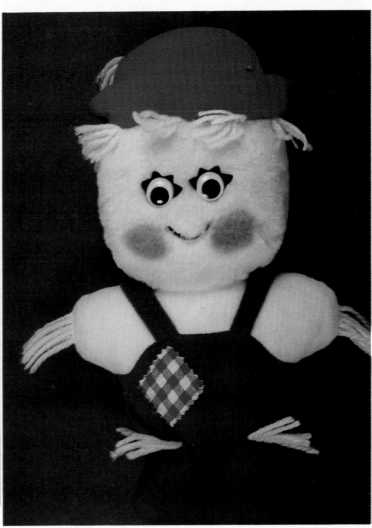

The Del Monte Shoo Shoo Scarecrow, 1983 ($10)

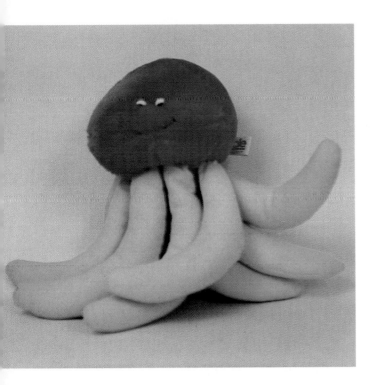

Bananapus

Del Monte Country Yumkin fruits: Lushie Peach from 1982 and Juicy Pineapple from 1983. ($10 each)

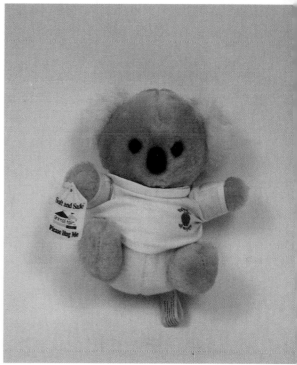

Country Yumkin Veggies:.Sweetie Pea, 1982, and Snappy Bean, 1983, were popular promotions. Other dolls in the series were Country Strawberry, 1989; Reddy Tomato, 1982, and Cobbie Corn, 1982. Fluffy Lamb and Cocky Crow were offered in 1984 and Yumkin Brawny Bear was offered in 1985.

The Mott Bear ($10)

Birdseye Chef ($15)

The Joy detergent Lemon fresh ($10)

The M&M Fun Friends were first offered as a Christmas offer in 1988. Mars M&M's were in the "C" rations of American soldiers during World War II and on the first space shuttle. ($10)

The Mott Elephant ($10)

Mars M&M Fun Friend

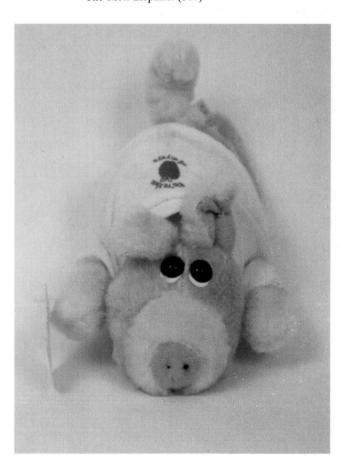

Mott's "You're the Apple of My Eye" pig ($10)

The Cajun Gator ($10)

Pip the Mouse, the Allentown, Pennsylvania, Downtown Improvement District Authority Christmas mouse. ($10)

Macy's Snoopy dog ($10)

Virgin Airlines Pilot Bird ($10)

The Isotoner Puppy ($10)

The Alpo puppy ($250

True Temper Eager Beaver ($65)

Notice the personalized dog tag.

Ford Motor Company St. Bernard ($15)

Cheers Detergent Cheeroo Kangeroo ($15)

The Quik Rabbit represented Nestle's
chocolate in 1976. ($35)

Chapter 11
Plastic and Vinyl Create New Playthings

The California Raisins are among the most popular vinyl creations in the advertising world. The Raisins made their debut in claymation in the 1980s to promote raisins as a healthy snack food. The inspiration for their characters was an old Motown tune "I Heard It Through the Grapevine," by Marvin Gaye. The Raisins' remake became an instant hit. Millions fell in love with these dancing raisins who sang soul music, strutted their stuff, and played jazz music. One of their best-selling promotions was a plastic California raisin sandwich that played the "Grapevine" hit.

Before California Raisins, the dried fruit was promoted by the Sun Maid Raisin girl. The original Sun Maid Raisin girl was a young Fresno girl named Lorraine Collett. One day Collett was sitting in her backyard, wearing a red bonnet. A group of Raisin executives passed by and saw her in her bonnet. They were entranced by the sight of the young girl with her long brunette curls and red bonnet and thus the trademark image was born. Collett was paid $15 a week to pose as the California Raisin girl. The name Sun Maid was a pun for sun made, referring to the fact that grapes, when dried in the sun, become raisins. One of the first things Collett did was to pose for a picture holding a tray of grapes. Another assignment was to accompany two other young women chosen to be representatives of the California Associated Raisin Company to the 1915 Panama-Pacific Exposition in San Francisco to help popularize raisins. In another promotions, she was asked to fly in a small airplane and drop raisins over crowds of people at various state fairs. Originally the Sun Maid Raisin girls wore blue bonnets.

Today both the Sun Maid Raisin girls and the California Raisins advertise the raisin industry. The California Raisins became an official trademark of the California Raisin Advisory Board in 1986. Designer Will Vinton created the claymation versions in 1987. The California Raisins also advertised Post Raisin Bran and were given out as promotions at Hardee's Fast Food Restaurants.

Before long other companies created small, pocket-sized vinyl and plastic collectibles. Campbell's Wizard of O's, the Magic Chef, and the Keebler Elf are only a few. As vinyl became more popular, more companies turned their trademarks into vinyl. Among the most commonly found are the Doughboy, Big Boy, Ronald McDonald, Little Sprout, Snap, Crackle, and Pop and the Campbell Kids.

This book has attempted to list many of the most common advertising dolls found in cloth form. Other dolls popular among collectors are the 1930s Black Jack Gum Rabbit, Baby Ruth, the 1950s Speedy Alka Seltzer, the 1964 Brer Rabbit Molasses Rabbit, and the 1959 Exxon Tiger. Many others exist in vinyl, plush, and plastic — such as the 1961 Mr. Clean, the 1976 Dunkin' Donuts Munchkin, numerous forms of Colonel Sanders, Gorton's Codfish Fisherman, Marky Maypo, the Pepto Bismol bug, and the Energizer Bunny.

Collecting advertising dolls is still a wonderful hobby because advertising dolls are a phenomena that are here to stay. Almost every day a new one appears on the market and, for the ardent collector, life can become a constant scavenger hunt with rewards waiting around almost every corner. Would-be collectors on small budgets can have a field day and enjoy the hunt. Whereas the original collectors had to stay at home and wait for the mail after sending off their box tops, since the first advertising dolls were mostly mail-in premium offers, today's dolls are more apt to be found in novelty stores, gift shops, and at fast food restaurants.

For the past twenty years, Christmas has been one of the most prolific seasons for a collector. This year alone there were new Coca Cola polar bears, new Sugar bears, and more Ronald McDonald collectibles. As always, Teddy bears remain one of the most popular forms of advertising dolls and cloth is still the most frequently used material. But since the 1980s, vinyl and plush have become close seconds.

Mars Candies' M&M Sport Dispenser
($25)

Out of the box.

A California Raisin ($10)

Sun Maid Wagon bank ($35)

More California Raisins

1975 Ralston Purina chuck wagon advertised Purina's Chuck Wagon
Dog Food. ($35)

Flintstone Vitamins bottles ($10 each)

The image of the Magic Chef has been used as a corporate logo for the American Stove Company since 1939. He was dressed in formal attire, with a black bow and a chef's hat. In 1951, the company changed its name to that of its imaginary promoter, becoming Magic Chef, Inc. ($55)

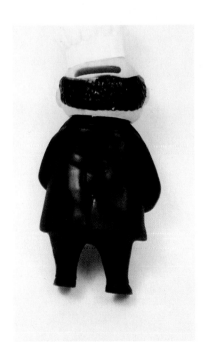

This Magic Chef is a bank.

The Stay-puff laundry detergent man is modeled after a character in the movie "Ghostbusters." ($25)

Marty Mayrose is an old-fashioned looking butcher who was manufactured in 1973 to advertise Swift and Company's Mayrose bacon. ($60)

The Poppin' Fresh family

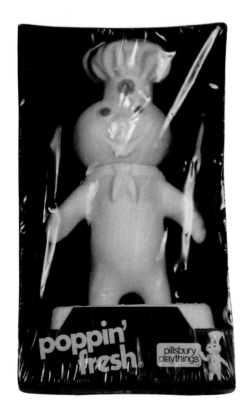

Poppin' fresh ($10 for the little ones.)

Poppin' Fresh puppet ($20)

Little Sprout ($10)

"You make me laugh, I like the Sprite in you," says Sprite's Lucky Lymon, the Sprite who made his first appearance in the 1990s. ($25)

Big Boy squeeze toy ($25)

Big Boy night light ($75)

Campbell's Wizard of O's advertises SphaghettiOs and was first offered in 1978 or 1979. ($25)

Ernie the Keebler Elf was issued in 1974. ($25)

The Swedish Chef ($30)

A Mickey Mouse cup promoting Disneyland
($15)

A Hallmark Christmas Keepsake

DC Card's frog

Bibliography

There are bits and pieces of information on advertising dolls in most doll books. But there are no detailed references to antique advertising icons in the many collectible books of advertising characters.

The bible for all advertising doll collectors is the now out of print — "Advertising Dolls: Identification & Value Guide" by Joleen Robison and Kay Sellers, Collector Books, 1983. Unfortunately Mrs. Robison died a few years ago and I was unable to locate Kay Sellers. Mrs. Robison's collection was dispersed as was one of her most important sources, Ralph's Antique Dolls.

Johanna Gast Anderton, *The Collector's Encyclopedia of Cloth Dolls*, Wallace and Homestead, 1984.

DollReader magazine has had many articles on individual dolls.

Warren Dotz, *Advertising Character Collectibles: An Identification and Value Guide*, Collectors Books, 1993.

Caroline Goodfellow, "The Ultimate Doll Book," Dorling Kindersley, 1994.

Polly and Pam Judd, *Composition Dolls —1928-1955*, 1991, Hobby House Press.

Mary Jane Lamphier, *Zany Characters of the Ad World: An Identification and Value Guide*, Collectors Books, 1995.

Myla Perkins, *Black Dolls: An Identification and Value Guide*, Collectors Books, 1995.

Rhode Island Historical Society, *Dolls and Duty: Martha Chase and the Progressive Agenda —1889-1925*, 1989.

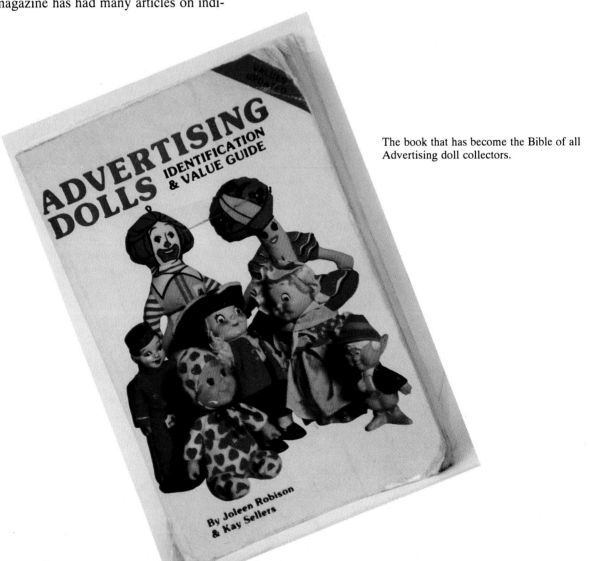

The book that has become the Bible of all Advertising doll collectors.